CHOOSING

PEACE

DEVOTIONALS

TRACI KECK

ISBN 978-1-68526-392-8 (Paperback)
ISBN 978-1-68526-393-5 (Digital)

Covenant Books
11661 Hwy 707
Murrells Inlet, SC 29576
www.covenantbooks.com

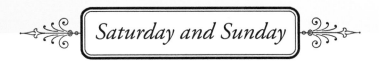

Saturday and Sunday

Let them turn away from evil and do good;
let them seek peace and pursue it.

—1 Peter 3:11

Choosing peace—where do we start you may be wondering.

Choosing is to pursue—and finding or making peace will not always be easy. We may have to search, face conflict, be uncomfortable with choices; that's the natural path. However, turning from negative inclinations to do good and make peace happen is more difficult.

Peace is a stress-free state, secure, calm—no fighting or war. Everyone coexists in perfect harmony and freedom. Are *you* still "choosing *peace*"? Peace can be small or big, seen in brief moments or entire countries.

What is peace to you? Reflect for a moment on the magnitude of your choice. When I was much younger, I wanted world peace so badly. I lived it, breathed it. I wore it on my shirts, wrote it on my books, journals, etc. Those who knew me knew what I was choosing.

Then I started experiencing life and lost that passion for world peace. I got caught up in the reality of what a monumental feat that would be for me by myself. I didn't shout it to the world around me because they would think it was ridiculous. Now, as I experience life more, I know I still want world peace. I want to love my neighbor, not fear for our children, get along, accept everyone for the beautiful soul that they are. How do I choose that?

I realize now that if I start with a moment of peace and if you start with a moment of peace, we can start making *peace* a beautiful reality. I encourage you this weekend to write down where you want to choose peace. Maybe love yourself for a minute and know it's okay. Maybe be kind to a stranger. Maybe let someone know you accept them unconditionally. Maybe pray for those that are hard to coexist with.

Peace will always be the more difficult choice, but that's what God has called us to do. That is the path for all of us—family, brothers, sisters, and strangers. Maybe I should choose *peace* on a smaller scale initially—peace with myself, my family, my neighbors, my community.

Where should you start?

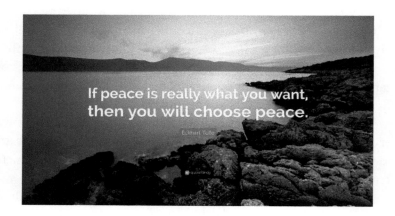

Monday

Trust in the Lord with all of your heart and do not lean
on your own understanding. In all your ways acknowledge
Him, and He will make your paths straight.

—Proverbs 3:5–6

Do you feel sometimes like you took a wrong turn? Maybe took the
long way around something? How in the heck did I get to this point
in my life? Me too.

I have taken paths I shouldn't have and always ended up okay. I
have made choices that were probably not the right ones and always
ended up okay. There are times in our lives where we look back and
think about how different life would be if only we had done something another way.

Take a moment today and reflect on something in your life
that you feel may have set you back. When you have that experience
in your mind, let go of any frustration and disappointment that is
attached to it. Instead, think of the good that came from that wrong
turn. What did you learn from it? Who might be in your life because
of it? How did it make you grow?

Trust in God that he is making your route easier than it would
be if you took it alone. Trust yourself that there is a reason even if
you don't know what it is yet. Sometimes taking the crooked, curvy,
winding path is the best route. God gives us opportunities to experience life in many ways. We get to choose the paths we want to take.
I truly believe God has a path for me, and I see purpose from the
"wrong" paths. I wasn't alone and always ended up okay.

Tuesday

May the Lord give strength to his people! May
the Lord bless his people with peace!
—Psalm 29:11

Struggle is good! I want to fly!

Once a little boy was playing outdoors and found a fascinating caterpillar. He carefully picked it up and took it home to show his mother. He asked his mother if he could keep it, and she said he could if he would take good care of it.

The little boy got a large jar from his mother and put plants to eat and a stick to climb on in the jar. Every day he watched the caterpillar and brought it new plants to eat.

One day, the caterpillar climbed up the stick and started acting strangely. The boy worriedly called his mother, who came and understood that the caterpillar was creating a cocoon. The mother explained to the boy how the caterpillar was going to go through a metamorphosis and become a butterfly.

The little boy was thrilled to hear about the changes his caterpillar would go through. He watched every day, waiting for the butterfly to emerge. One day it happened—a small hole appeared in the cocoon, and the butterfly started to struggle to come out.

At first the boy was excited, but soon he became concerned. The butterfly was struggling so hard to get out! It looked like it couldn't break free! It looked desperate! It looked like it was making no progress!

The boy was so concerned he decided to help. He ran to get scissors and then walked back (because he had learned not to run with scissors). He snipped the cocoon to make the hole bigger, and the butterfly quickly emerged!

As the butterfly came out, the boy was surprised. It had a swollen body and small shriveled wings. He continued to watch the butterfly expecting that at any moment the wings would dry out, enlarge, and expand to support the swollen body. He knew that in time the body would shrink and the butterfly's wings would expand.

But neither happened! The butterfly spent the rest of its life crawling around with a swollen body and shriveled wings. It never was able to fly.

As the boy tried to figure out what had gone wrong, his mother took him to talk to a scientist from a local college. He learned that the butterfly was *supposed* to struggle. In fact, the butterfly's struggle to push its way through the tiny opening of the cocoon pushes the fluid out of its body and into its wings. Without the struggle, the butterfly would never, ever fly. The boy's good intentions hurt the butterfly.

This story has been around for a long time. It's been used in schools to encourage kids to keep working toward their goals, used for athletes, for everyone. It is an example of that sometimes God allows struggles in our lives to help us reach our true potential.

Our struggles in life help us to develop our strengths. Without struggles, we never grow and get stronger, so it's important for us to tackle challenges. As you go through life, keep in mind that struggling is an important part of any growth experience. In fact, it is the struggle that causes you to develop your ability to fly.

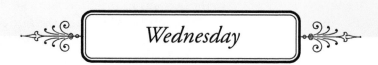

Wednesday

Dear children, let us not love with words or
speech but with actions and in truth.

—1 John 3:18

Did you grow up volunteering for things? With your family, your church, your school? Were you on the receiving end of someone serving? Or maybe serving wasn't a part of your life.

I got my passion for serving because people helped my family when I was younger. My mom was late picking us up from the babysitter one evening. Came to find out we lost our home in a fire that day. No one was home; therefore, no one was hurt—thank you God.

Everything else was lost.

People didn't know us; we didn't know them. They knew a hardworking mom with six kids between three and fifteen years old had just lost everything. I remember it was devastating and sad, but we kept going. We stayed with friends and were given clothes and food, and the list goes on. I don't remember feeling I went without because of the kindness of countless strangers.

Now as an adult, I serve. My family serves. I want my children to understand there is always a need from someone and we can help. We help serve the Thanksgiving meal at church. We donate clothes and toys. My son goes on mission trips with his youth group to help other people. We help with events at church, at school, etc.

When my daughter decided to donate some of her Barbies because even though she liked them, she thought another little girl might enjoy playing with them more—my heart was full (and proud).

In our quest for *peace*, we have to teach and include the young people in our communities. They have to be a part of filling this world with love by their actions. One little person at a time can make a difference.

I encourage you to look for one way to serve with your children or with youth in your community—it'll be a great start!

We can serve!

Thursday

The message you heard from the very beginning
is this: we must love one another.

—1 John 3:11

Free hugs

I like to think that giving a hug is a great way to show love for one another. It is scientifically proven to do so much good for us. Here are five things it does:

1. Balances the nervous system
2. Reduces stress levels
3. Better overall mood
4. Relaxes your body
5. Heart health improves/decreases heart rate

Hugging someone can ease a majority of their stress immediately and effectively. Too often we underestimate the power of hugging.

What happens is that when being hugged, the level of cortisol that is circulating throughout our body is reduced tremendously. This means that our minds are able to calm down and think without stress.

Hugging has the amazing ability to decrease our heart rate. A study brought to light by the University of North Carolina Chapel Hill suggested that the volunteers who had little to no contact at all with their partners had developed a much faster heart rate of ten beats per minute compared to the standard five beats per minute of those who were hugged by their partner all the time.

We need to be hugging each other every single day for our mental and physical health—more importantly our happiness. Do you want to stress less, sleep better, and feel abundantly happier without drugs or anything crazy? Are you feeling a little stressed? Then give hugs—you most always receive one back!

Hugging
is good medicine.
It transfers energy
and gives the person
hugged an emotional lift.
*You need four hugs
a day for survival,
eight for maintenance,
and twelve for growth.*
Scientists say that
hugging is a form of
communication because
it can say things you
don't have the words for.
And the nicest thing
about a hug is that
you usually can't give
one without getting one.

share to your love ones ♡

Friday

Blessed are those who mourn, for they will be comforted.
—Matthew 5:4

Mourning or grieving is the natural response to a loss. The significance of the loss in part determines the intensity of the mourning. Death of a loved one is often the cause of the most intense mourning. There are many other kinds of loss that people experience: divorce, loss of security, loss of health, loss of a pet, a miscarriage, loss of a friendship, loss of a home—to name a few. All are of value and worthy of grieving.

Accepting your grief is important. It is okay to grieve, and it is a different process for everyone. There is no right or wrong way, no set amount of time. How do we find comfort in mourning?

No matter what you are mourning, try to trust that you are not alone. Others may be grieving with you, others may have been through something similar, so reach out when you can. Don't withdraw too much from those around you. Sharing stories, memories, things that helped you get through yesterday—it's important to talk about your feelings to get to a place of peace with a loss.

You may draw comfort from friends and family, a support group, your faith (prayer and Scripture), or a counselor or therapist. These are all okay and accepted and comforting. God will comfort you with memories and signs when you really need them—pictures, songs, stories you hadn't heard. These things will help.

Take care of yourself as much as you can. Some days may be easier than others. Rest, take a walk, pray, and know that whatever you are feeling is okay. And when you are ready, seek peace.

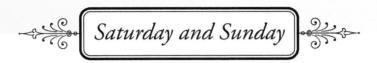

Saturday and Sunday

Clap your hands, all you peoples; shout
to God with loud songs of joy.

—Psalm 47:1

Are you feeling joy today? Do you feel happiness? There are many synonyms for *joy*: delight, great pleasure, joyfulness, jubilation, triumph, exultation, rejoicing, happiness, gladness, glee, exhilaration, ebullience, exuberance, elation, euphoria, bliss, ecstasy, transports of delight, rapture, radiance—any of those feels right now?

What is the spiritual meaning of *joy*?

Webster's defines *joy* as "the emotion evoked by well-being, success, or good fortune or by the prospect of possessing what one desires." Similarly, John Piper writes, "Christian joy is a good feeling in the soul, produced by the Holy Spirit, as he causes us to see the beauty of Christ in the word and in the world" (August 3, 2017).

How are the two of these connected in your life? And if they are not, how can you connect them? If I stop to just enjoy what is "right there," I can feel the emotion of finding joy. For example, driving to work—sometimes it has been a crazy morning: kids aren't moving quick, dog doesn't want to come in, back in the house for whatever is forgotten, then traffic construction, every light is red—you know that morning, right? Then I look around me (sitting at one of those red lights), and there is a rainbow connecting one side of the city to the other side, and in that moment, I smile and feel something in my soul reminding me there is purpose and it's all going to be fine today.

Where do you find joy? Swimming, hiking, spending time with family and friends, building a fire, going to the lake, baking cookies, reading a book, listening to music—-whatever it is, do it this weekend! If it's a busy weekend, work, sporting events, etc., then think about how you can find joy in what you have to do. If you have to spend the weekend at soccer games or baseball games, find joy in the face of the kids who scored, the grandparents that are proud—you get it!

Put yourself in places and moments that bring you joy It's a great feeling!

Monday

I can do all things in Him who strengthens me.
—Philippians 4:13

When you think about doing good and trying your best to make a difference in the world, who are you doing it for? For your family, your neighbors, your state, your country, the world, or for yourself? More often than not, the reasons are for one of the first couple of choices, almost never for ourselves.

But we should do it for ourselves. It starts with you. If you don't feel worthy of peace and find that peace for yourself, then how can you possibly find it and bring it about for others? This is a common thread in all our lives.

In our selflessness, we want for everyone else. We think we need to fix things for everyone else. It is really easy to live that mindset daily. To naturally care for others is normal for many of you, and that is part of what we need for success in our lives.

However, in choosing peace, make sure to also choose it for *you*! Yes, *you*! You deserve it. You need it. Believe that whatever you do is going to be a step toward choosing goodness.

Sometimes we make decisions that are tough, not-so-fun choices. People get frustrated and tell you you're wrong, that was a bad idea, etc. Before you change your mind, take a moment to think about why you made the choice you did. Was it to keep someone safe? Was it more inclusive to everyone involved? Was it faster, less expensive, etc.? Believe in yourself and the choices you make, and stick with them.

Believing in yourself is not easy but very important! God is with you already paving the way to your greatness. Live it, and believe in it!

Tuesday

Give thanks in all circumstances; for this is the
will of God in Christ Jesus for you.

—1 Thessalonians 5:18

Giving thanks sounds easy, but do we always remember that?

Gratitude is an emotion expressing appreciation for what one has—a readiness to be thankful and return kindness. Have you thought about the science of gratitude? There are endless benefits to being thankful: having more positive emotions, feeling present in the world, getting a good night sleep. You may express more compassion and kindness, which all help you feel healthier.

Research by UC Davis psychologist Robert Emmons, author of *Thanks! How the New Science of Gratitude Can Make You Happier*, shows that simply keeping a gratitude journal—regularly writing brief reflections on moments for which we're thankful—can significantly increase well-being and life satisfaction.

Now you would think the benefits named or the research stated above would all be enough to motivate you to increase your practice of gratitude—but life tends to interrupt even the best plans or ideas. So, starting small counts and doesn't seem like such a big task.

Here are some things you can start doing this week to begin to really reap the benefits of gratitude:

- Be aware of what you are thankful for. Instead of being thankful just for my family, I am thankful for the little message my sister sent me that brightened my day.

- Be real about starting this new practice of gratitude (whether it is journaling, conscious list, etc.) by acknowledging possible obstacles. For example, if you are going to journal at night and you work until midnight, plan ahead and do it early that day. Don't blame your schedule for throwing you off course.
- Make it fun and creative. You could have a gratitude jar. Anytime something happens that you appreciate or are grateful for, write it down, and put it in the jar. Pick a special time to look at your year of gratitude (New Year's Eve, birthday, when you're feeling down, etc.). Great family activity!
- Let people know when you are grateful for something they did!

These are just a few ways to practice gratitude! Brainstorm ideas, and start putting into practice something today. God is good, and there is so much good even in the bad we see in our world. Sometimes we have to be reminded and stop and look for it, but if we practice this—giving thanks is good!

Wednesday

Be strong and of good courage, do not fear nor be afraid
of them; for the LORD your God, He is the One who goes
with you. He will not leave you nor forsake you.
—Deuteronomy 31:6

Feeling overwhelmed? Is there a mountain just too big to climb in your life? Is there so much going on that you can't possibly face it alone? Do not fear the unknown? You can do this one step at a time—and you are not alone.

Life is busy, stressful, overwhelming, and sometimes we get caught up in trying to see the end and giving up because it is so far away. Other times, we have no idea what the end is, so we fear the unknown and quit trying.

There are many situations that people encounter in their lives that require courage. What we don't realize is that "courage" is being brave and being able to face something that is frightening. How many examples can you think of in your life right now this morning? Stop and think about it for a moment:

- Do you know someone fighting cancer?
- Do you know someone caring for the elderly?
- Do you know someone who is learning to ride a bike?
- Do you know someone "coming out"?
- Do you know someone looking for somewhere to sleep tonight?
- Do you know someone who is choosing *peace*?
- Or maybe you are that someone?

These are all examples of things that require courage, and when you think of these things, nobody does any of those things alone—not really. Most often, there is an army of support from friends, family, books, prayers, and God. God sometimes is carrying you through the treatment, providing shelter over you, or holding your hand, giving you signs for the path he has laid out for you. Have faith, and be courageous.

I found a great blog that gives a lot of examples about courage that you should check out when you have time—Lion's Whiskers: The Six Types of Courage. There is also an Ethiopian folktale by Nancy Raines Day called The Lion's Whisker. Both of these teach you something about what you are afraid of, and when you learn the unknown—it's not so scary anymore.

Thursday

Not that I am speaking of being in need, for I have
learned in whatever situation I am to be content.
—Philippians 4:11

Are you looking for a magic way to find balance in your life? Are you performing a daily juggling act just to get by? Take a breath—you are not alone. Life is happening, and we are all trying to find balance between work, home, family, friends, etc.

Stop worrying. Live your life the best you can. Live the way God has called you to live, and you will find balance. God can "tip the scales" in relation to us. However, how we respond to that will help us find our balance.

There are many things we can do to create a feeling of balance: have a schedule, stick to a routine, make time for everyone, plan ahead—all great when things happen the way you expect them to. How do we get that feeling when they don't go as planned?

Here are a few things to start incorporating into your already busy life: feed your body and soul (eat breakfast, and read a devotional), exercise your body and soul (maybe take a walk and listen to worship music), give yourself a certain amount of time for chores, and then stop (it'll be there tomorrow), say *no* to something if you are already overwhelmed (it's okay), and most importantly, take a day off. God created a Sabbath day for a reason—practice using it. Sunday might not work for you, but try and find one that does.

Look at your life. Keep the things in it that feed your soul and make you happy. Create some space for finding balance and feeling peace. If you are reading this—you're off to a good start!

Friday

But if we hope for what we do not see, we wait for it with patience.
—Romans 8:25

Patience is a challenging quality to maintain in the sometimes cha-otic world we live in. To have the ability to be calm, accept whatever comes up—it is a daily commitment. There are many references to patience in Scripture implying suffering, waiting without complain-ing, enduring injustices, and in doing so, grace will be yours in so many ways.

There are a lot of examples of being impatient. As a parent, I have to remember that things aren't always going to be done the way I would do them. When I teach my children a chore, I have to make myself stand back and let my kids do it and maybe show them how to do something more than once. I have to allow them to put their own spin on it.

As an employee, I have to remember to delegate to other employees, to allow them the opportunity to learn and grow even it that process takes longer.

As a spouse, I have to acknowledge that people think and do differently, and that's okay. I have to embrace those differences and know that's what creates a balance in our home—to not all be the same.

All these examples have something in common—learning from each other. We must teach others to create the peace we are looking for. We must love each other and endure the time it takes for some-one to learn and gain an understanding of something. Kids will help with chores, employees will share the workload, partners will have a better understanding of each other—all worthy benefits of patience.

So take a deep breath, say a little prayer, and wait for the goodness to happen. Have faith—it will happen!

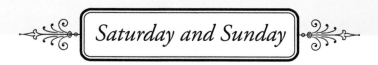

Saturday and Sunday

Keep alert, stand firm in your faith, be courageous, be strong.
—1 Corinthians 16:13

A father's love

What do we know about "a father's love"? Father's Day was always really hard and strange for me growing up. I never lived with my dad; my parents were separated shortly before I was born. I knew my dad, and we loved each other, but there wasn't a lot of connecting and life lessons that came from that relationship.

My grandpa was my fatherly role model—strong, courageous, compassionate and even-tempered and so loving and patient. He even gave me away (agreed to share me) when I was married. It was like he read what God wanted and did it—he lived it! My grandpa had five children, twenty-two grandchildren, forty-two great-grandchildren, and one great-great grandchild at the time of his death and he made every single one of us feel like the most important person in his life and it was always that way.

We are called to teach our children right from wrong, love them unconditionally, be strong, provide for them, play with them, make good choices for them, and support them in making their own choices and then lifting them up when sometimes those don't work out. Those are just a few things "fathers" do. So much pressure! Some can handle the pressure—and some can't.

It wasn't until my dad was dying that I learned how much he really loved me even though he didn't know how to show me. He was so proud of me and my siblings, and everyone in his community knew how much he loved us and how proud of us he was all along. He did the best he could do—and God knew that too. Sometimes we don't know what we can't see.

Support the fathers out there that you know! Encourage them, love them, and pray with them. God is with them every step of the way. Don't judge them for what they can't do; just support them and help them recognize what they can do, and have role models in their lives that help with the rest—that Father in the image of God.

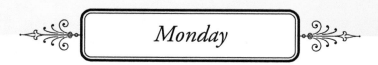

Monday

Now faith is confidence in what we hope for
and assurance about what we do not see.

—Hebrews 11:1

Do you believe in your choices? Do you have faith that things will happen the way you planned? Or do you sometimes get lost in the commotion and quit trying?

Think of something you really want to happen—an exercise program, buy a new home, volunteer monthly, visit a friend, or strive for peace. There may be more than one thing. What is your goal?

Write down your goal; visualize it too. "What you think about, you bring about." Tell your friends or family about it. Having a good support team helps build confidence. Now that's where you start—next is baby steps to get there!

What are the things that need to happen to get there, the steps to take, the actions? Make a list of every little step or a chart. Make something visual because as you cross things off the list, you will see the progress. The confidence you build will be as powerful as achieving the end goal.

God knows we will have struggles, that we will have doubts along the way. Verses like the one above are for those moments. Use them during your time of doubt, and pray through it! Believe in yourself. "If you believe it, you can achieve it!"

Tuesday

Stand firm, and you will win life.

—Luke 21:19

Perseverance is defined as the persistence in doing something despite difficulty or delay in achieving success, never giving up no matter what the odds are of achieving the task. What are the odds of finding peace, you may wonder? To some, it sounds ridiculous, outrageous. Why waste your time? It is worth it to me!

Do I want *peace* everywhere? Of course I do! But I will start with right here. How often do we give up on something because it is hard? People quit smoking or quit drinking—and start back up again. Too many triggers or reminders to have to struggle with. People quit that exercise routine; it made them sore. People stop trying to make something work because it is too much work. We've all been here.

Have you been at the other end of the spectrum? You had perseverance and stuck it out, never quit, what an amazing accomplishment!! How did you do that? What steps helped you do it? Please share your story (stories) of perseverance with people. Someone is at the beginning of what you have achieved. Be proud of yourself!

I'm including one of my favorite stories about perseverance, The Story of the Bumblebee. It's factual and magical, and that seems to reflect real life a little bit. Basically, despite all impossibilities or odds, you can "fly" if you try hard enough!

> Aerodynamically, the bumble bee shouldn't be able to fly, but the bumble bee doesn't know it so it goes on flying anyway.
>
> - Mary Kay Ash

Wednesday

Whoever is slow to anger has great understanding,
but one who has a hasty temper exalts folly.
—Proverbs 14:29

Peace can come about—if we allow ourselves to understand what is preventing it. This is true for our world, our country, our state, our community, our family and friends, and even ourselves. If you are choosing peace, then choose to understand the conflict in yourself and in your community to begin getting there.

We all have the ability to judge a situation, but can you do so without judgment? For example, a kindergarten teacher had the most caring way to teach positive behavior to new little students. She was teaching the students to walk single file, keep their hands to themselves, be quiet—normal school behavior. She told the parents that she had a lot of tolerance because she knew she was asking them to do something they had never done before. She knew it made sense to her but would take practice for them. She had an understanding that their little young minds did not think the same as hers.

When I heard that story, it was an aha moment that can be applied to all situations that are frustrating or hard to understand. The key to achieving this understanding was not to expect them to think like her but to actually understand them and find a way to teach them something they didn't know.

One of the hard parts of "understanding" is we get so caught up in why people don't understand us that we don't listen and look at where the misunderstanding is…it is almost always not personal. We are all different. We were created to be our own person. We don't have to let go of what we know or believe to be true; we just also have to be accepting of learning or acknowledging another way sometimes.

To understand is really having a positive relationship and the ability to have an informal agreement—to be kind and caring. When we are open to working together and learning from each other, we will find similarities. Learning how to learn from each other has a lot to do with survival and peace.

Thursday

Now Sarah said, "God has brought laughter for me;
everyone who hears will laugh with me."
—Genesis 21:6

Laughter is timeless. Imagination has no age. And dreams are forever. (Walt Disney)

A day without laughter is a day wasted. (Charlie Chaplin)

Laughter is the best medicine.

I love people who make me laugh. I honestly think it's the thing I like most, to laugh. It cures a multitude of ills. It's probably the most important thing in a person. (Audrey Hepburn)

Laughter is God's blessing. (Joseph Prince)

Do any of these quotes sound familiar? Hopefully, they have all deemed to be true at one time or another. Laughter is good medicine It also just might be the most contagious of all emotional experiences. Scientists do know that laughter is a highly sophisticated social signaling system, helping people bond and even negotiate. Interestingly, most social laughter does not result from any obvious joke. Sometimes it can be triggered by embarrassment and other social discomforts, or sometimes it is better than crying. Laughter may have evolved to facilitate bonding across large groups of people. It enables us to bond quickly and easily with a large community.

Has anything ever just struck you funny—so funny you start laughing uncontrollably, and you can't even tell anyone what it was (because you are laughing so hard)? Then when you can tell them, they look at you like it wasn't funny at all. Didn't it feel great to laugh so hard? The release of such intense positive emotion is incredible! How can we get to that positive release more often?

There are so many benefits of laughter: boost the immune system, relax muscles, aid circulation, and protect against heart disease. It's good for your mental health too. Laughter can lower anxiety, release tension, and can improve your mood. Laughter can strengthen a relationship by helping to defuse conflict and allowing people to successfully operate as a team. The benefits are worth a convulsive fit of laughing once in a while.

In the process of finding peace, do you wonder what would happen if we discussed differences with positive energy, smiles, and a few laughs? What is the worst that can happen? We might find that cracking a smile makes all the tension in the room disappear. We may find that we have something in common—this human emotion.

We all have rough days, some more than others. Do you have someone who tries to cheer you up? Are you someone who tries to do the cheering up? Maybe you're a "glass half empty" instead of a "glass half full" person.

Either one is okay, but recognize which one you are and then take steps to fill your glass. I challenge you all to send the picture below to someone today (or this week) that really needs to stop and just laugh or any other thing that you think will crack someone up.

I think you will, in return, get the response that helps you on your journey to some peace.

https://www.helpguide.org/articles/mental-health/laughter-is-the-best-medicine.htm

Friday

I pray that, according to the riches of his glory, he
may grant that you may be strengthened in your
inner being with power through his Spirit.

—Ephesians 3:16

So often when we think of strength and power, we think of physical strength.

Physical strength is important, but our inner strength is far more powerful. And when we are stressed, grieving, in despair, confused, or even tired, our inner power can feel very weak. Finding ways to revive that inner strength is important in surviving the negative things in the world we live in right now.

There are so many people suffering silently right now; we had someone in our church community reach out to us and make herself very vulnerable. She was feeling weak, defeated. Her family has suffered four deaths due to gun violence recently. It is not just happening to someone we don't know. She is tired of pretending that "she's got this."

We need to make ourselves available to people. We need to let people "in" our lives and help each other. Her weakness is an extreme example but relevant in our communities today. You may know other people feeling weak, people who work sixty hours a week just to make ends meet, kids raising their siblings so someone can work all the time, someone whose car broke down, or someone fighting cancer.

Reach out to people in your lives, and check on them! Yes, still tell them "they got this," but also ask what you can do to help them "get it"—maybe watching their kids for one hour so they can go to the store by themselves, maybe inviting someone over to your house for dinner and talking, offering a ride, inviting them to church, sending them a devotional that just might remind them that they are loved and not alone.

In our very busy, lively, chaotic lives is a community that is the same way, in a country that is the same way, and we need to take time to breathe and be present in each other's lives to help each other breathe. Things are still going to happen, we need to help each other get through, and in doing so, take in some powerful breaths that help us be strong!

> Life is not about waiting for the storms to
> pass. It's about learning how to dance in the rain.
> (Vivian Greene)

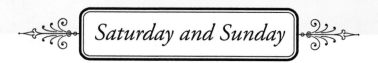

Saturday and Sunday

Fear not, for I am with you; Be not dismayed, for I am
your God. I will strengthen you, Yes, I will help you,
I will uphold you with My righteous right hand.

—Isaiah 41:10

How do we find calm during the storms around us? Sometimes seeking shelter brings a sense of calm or protection. We put ourselves in a safe place with a sense of security until the storm passes. We can handle the "storms" in our lives or community the same way.

In this life we have two choices. We can go along with the tempo of our environment, letting our mind and emotions be led by the twists and turns of the ever-changing scenarios of life, or we can set our hearts and minds on something higher and stable for our soul. I'm choosing the latter.

I'm seeking serenity—the calm, peaceful joy you get when you trust and believe that everything is going to be all right, that this is in God's hands. There are things I can do to change the situation, and there are things that are God's.

When I don't waste my energy trying to blame what's happening on something else, I seem to have a lot more energy left over to change myself. If there is a decision we don't agree with, rather than focus on all the negative things that may come out of it, we can focus on the positive that may arise from it. When we work on changing how we look at something, we seem to have a lot less problems with it.

The storms of life can overwhelm and overpower us, so we need to seek serenity from God and receive it from him. Below is the

Serenity Prayer; it was written by the American theologian Reinhold Niebuhr. It is commonly used in support groups and various situations to help people identify what they need to do to find calm or peace during the storms of life. I encourage you to say it or read it daily. It really helps put in perspective how big the "storm" really is.

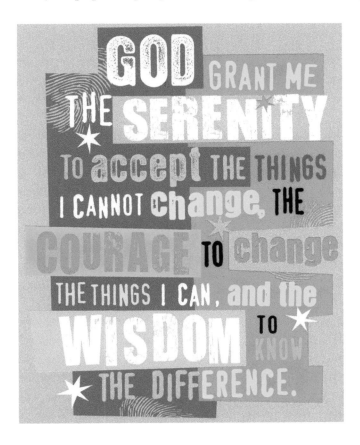

Monday

The Golden Rule: "In everything do to others as you would have them do to you; for this is the law and the prophets."
—Matthew 7:12

The Golden Rule ultimately inspires us to treat others with respect, kindness, and fairness. Like many principles of morals and manners, the Golden Rule is not absolute; it can help to be flexible and learn where exceptions might work better. Part of the difficulty in attaining peace is that everyone is not on the same page, and some people think that you should be on the same page to get there—let that thought go!

God created all people and created us all differently for a purpose and we might not always understand the reasons. Regardless of this, we must respect the differences in everyone. It is God's will.

We need to learn from each other, agree to disagree, love unconditionally. I bet everyone can think of someone they know who is different: maybe they are part of the LGBQT community, maybe they don't think of family and the way they support each other, maybe they don't eat meat, maybe they don't believe in the same politics, etc.

Rather than trying to change someone or undo who they are and what they think, we should respect them. We should love them for being who God intended them to be. We should learn what we can about who they are and how that can broaden our mindset and open us to possibilities. We need to remember that we don't have to agree with everyone's differences, but we do need to respect them. We each have a place, a purpose in this journey to peace. The sooner we spend energy on love, the sooner we find our way.

We will only get there by accepting and respecting everyone's differences.

Tuesday

May the God of hope fill you with all joy and peace in believing,
so that you may abound in hope by the power of the Holy Spirit.
—Romans 15:13

Feeling defeated or overwhelmed sometimes? That feeling of spending hours cleaning your house and you stop and look around—it's still dirty. You've explained something umpteen times, and it's still not understood. You're waiting in line for a ride at Disney World, and then it is shut down when you're up next. You are exercising, and the results don't come as fast as you want them to. We all feel that hopelessness sometimes.

Despite the obstacles and challenges we may experience, there is always an opportunity to choose love and rise above resentment and fear. The Bible was created to remind us of such truth and to encourage us to believe in the goodness of life and God.

There are also things we can do to choose hope:

- Try setting a goal that is challenging yet attainable. Clean one room at a time (without the pressure of the whole house needing to be clean), and visualize the results.
- Work steadily. God didn't create the world in one day. Don't give up—have patience.
- Share your goal(s) with your family or friends with someone who is encouraging but will also do accountability checks.
- Take care of yourself. Be nice to yourself.

- Meditate on this verse (or any other verse that speaks to you) through the day and share them with your friends so you can make an impact on someone else's day!

When you choose hope, it will literally open you up. Hope removes the blinders of fear and despair and will allow you to see the big picture.

Wednesday

Bear with one another and, if anyone has a complaint
against another, forgive each other; just as the Lord
has forgiven you, so you also must forgive.
—Colossians 3:13

Forgiving others is one of the hardest things to do. I haven't met a person yet who didn't go through something sometime in their life that is going to require some forgiveness. It is part of the world we live in—selfishness, greed, anger—all characteristics of things that cause pain.

Some people have gone through divorces, suffered different kinds of abuse, felt unloved from a parent, haven't been supported from their families, etc. Kids have been bullied, picked last for the team, abused, etc. We all face something, and we all have to learn to forgive.

God commands that we forgive others and extend grace as we have been shown grace. The pain and hurt others cause us is real and great, but the pain of living with bitterness and not forgiving can destroy you. When we forgive others, we are not saying what they did was okay, but we are releasing them to God and letting go of its hold on us.

My mom always said, "God doesn't give you more than you can handle." And sometimes, I really wondered why God thought I could handle so much. However, that statement always helped me to forgive and not hate. I knew I had to let it go, give it to God, and move on. I didn't like or agree with something, but I didn't want it poisoning my soul my whole life. I truly believe if God thought I could handle it, I could, and something good would come of it.

How do we forgive? You can actually tell someone you forgive them; you can just pray about it and tell God what it is you forgive; you can share with someone what you had been through and get it out of your head; you can write it down on paper and burn it—there are so many ways to forgive.

If you are carrying something deep inside that builds resentment, anger, stress, heartache, close your eyes, take a deep breath, and *let it go.*

It's time for you to choose your peace.

Thursday

Humble yourselves before the Lord, and he will lift you up.
—James 4:10

The one characteristic of authentic power that most people
overlook is humbleness. It is important for many reasons.
A humble person walks in a friendly world. He or she sees
friends everywhere he or she looks, wherever he or she
goes, whomever he or she meets. His or her perception
goes beyond the shell of appearance and into essence.
—Gary Zukav

What does it mean to be humble? Research demonstrates that humility is closely correlated with courage, integrity, strong leadership, self-control, learning, and better relationships. It is not to be boastful, selfish, prideful. It is the ability to learn from others and situations. It is kindness. It is helping others. Jesus is the best example of someone who humbly followed God's plan for his life.

Here are some characteristics of someone who is humble:

A humble person is teachable.
A humble person is at peace with themselves and others.
A humble person is grateful.
A humble person is slow to offend and quick to forgive.
A humble person asks for help.
A humble person treats everybody with respect.
A humble person is patient and doesn't easily get frustrated with
the imperfection of others.

A humble person recognizes their own limitations.
A humble person celebrates the accomplishments of others.
A humble person is open to a deep relationship with God.

In trying to be humble, we can start recognizing our strengths and passions in life. We can stop tearing ourselves down and have an accurate view of who we are instead of a negative view. When we recognize that, we can stop comparing ourselves to others and trying to be better than someone else. There is no competition in being the best you! We are all created uniquely and can all be humble.

Lori McKenna wrote a popular country song, "Humble and Kind." She merely wrote it as a message to her five children. She was trying to think of a way to give them a prayer of how to live life. She then sent the song to country music star Tim McGraw. It is a beautiful song about simply being a good person, whether you like country or not. It was very well written, and the video encompasses our world. It feels like it is a good fit for our journey to *peace*.

I hope you enjoy it!
bit.ly/34mNnd7

Friday

He answered, "If you have two shirts, share with someone who does not have one. If you have food, share that too."

—Luke 3:11

Caring for others is going on all around us! It is a good thing, and we need to do more of it. There are many ways we see it happening: feeding the hungry (donating to an organization or working in a soup kitchen or food pantry), caring for the elderly (taking care of a parent, singing at a nursing home, doing home visits), looking after children (volunteering at a camp, offering rides to kids that need one, teaching them), etc.

Caring is a very important part of bringing peace to our world. We need to be empathetic to strangers. What is their story and their need? When someone needs to talk, consciously listen to them, help them feel valued. When someone needs food, feed them and have food for later.

However, we all know there is stress related to caring as well. Caregivers can burn out, get exhausted (especially emotionally). It takes a lot to give and give, and there are many unspoken sacrifices. There are benefits to caring, and remembering these benefits will help caregivers continue to do what they do—to take care of people, to continue to volunteer, to reach out to those in need.

Some of the benefits of caring:

1.   Helping others makes you feel better, happier. Volunteer for something, and see how you feel. Serving a meal or helping a child learn to read—both very rewarding.

2.	Helping others helps promote positive attitudes and behaviors in teenagers. Teens that spend some time focusing on others learn the value of what they have—not only material things but the relationships they are blessed to be a part of.
3.	Helping others helps give you a sense of purpose, takes the focus off what you have or need, and adds value to your goals.
4.	Helping others can give you a feeling of accomplishment. You learn skills that will always be with you.
5.	Helping others is giving back, and that feels good. When you share the ways in which you volunteer, other people want to do it too! It is so contagious. This positive energy.
6.	Helping others is what we are called to do! We are to support each other, lift each other up, praise each other, give hope to each other.

Caring is such a powerful tool in our world. The ability to show compassion for someone leads to courage and understanding. It can lead to strong relationships and trust. Understanding and trust can lead to peace!

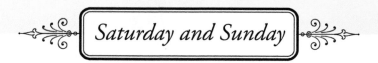

Saturday and Sunday

Make every effort to keep yourselves united in the
Spirit, binding yourselves together with peace.

—Ephesians 4:3

Wow, read that scripture again—simple and to the point, isn't it? Do your best, try your hardest, find some peace. Create unity together. It's not saying you have to agree with everyone or have the same point of view or do things the same way—just make every effort you can.

We easily get caught up in our thoughts, feelings, beliefs that we lose touch with the simple truth that it doesn't "completely" matter if we are alone. We need each other's differences to make this world go round. We should be open to what everyone has to offer to reach our goals.

A while back, there were twelve of us preparing to go on a mission trip to Puerto Rico. We represented two churches, one pastor, ages 21–71, and not everyone had met each other. We were getting ready to spend a week together on a hurricane-ravaged island with possibly no air conditioning, a translator to help us communicate and work side by side. Some would wonder how that could work out.

Our plans changed before we left the ground. Our flight was cancelled. In the next twenty-four hours, we all made it there on six different pathways, different airlines, and were greeted each time by loving people who couldn't believe we came to help them. This overcoming of challenges continued throughout the week. We accomplished more than they had hoped (or planned) for us to do in our short visit.

Both the translator and coordinator we worked with wondered how long we (as a group) had been working together. It had to be a long time. They felt and observed so much unity in our group that they couldn't believe some of us had barely met! You see, we merely focused on one goal—helping the people of Vieques recover from a devastating hurricane. That's it!

So as you look at the community around you or around your families, look at how you can "make every effort to be united in peace."

Monday

Finally, brothers and sisters, whatever is true, whatever
is noble, whatever is right, whatever is pure, whatever is
lovely, whatever is admirable—if anything is excellent or
praiseworthy—think about such things. 9 Whatever you have
learned or received or heard from me, or seen in me—put
it into practice. And the God of peace will be with you.
—Philippians 4:8–9

There is so much noise in the world around us today. How do we get through it to think? All around us are modes of unending information, entertainment, so much electronic clutter. We can get answers to just about anything, yet we forget how to have quiet and peace. With all the distractions and all that is happening in our world, we struggle with how to sift through it and focus on the good things to bring about peace.

Here are five things to help you find peace:

1. Find a quiet place.
2. Remove distractions.
3. Relax your body.
4. Concentrate on stillness.
5. Move beyond the present moment.

There are many steps and examples of these five things at wiki-How website: wikihow.com/Find-Peace#

It is up to each one of us to bring attention to the positive around us. We need to celebrate the good! Good things receive way too little air time. Share your stories of good will. Share with the kids around you when good things happen. Applaud them when they do good deeds; they are more likely to continue that behavior.

The thought of focusing on what is excellent or praiseworthy is an important task. How often do we lie awake at night, thinking about what is going wrong and could go wrong? We spend way too much negative energy on bad things. Take a moment at the end of each day jotting down on paper or in your head three good things. It seems hard at first. However, positive attracts positive. It will get easier. Maybe do it as a family thing at dinner or share with your friends.

You see where this is going? We are choosing to spread positive energy through the good things that are happening in the world around us. There is something good—a silver lining—to everything. Let's find it and share it.

Tuesday

So I tell you, whatever you ask for in prayer, believe
that you have received it, and it will be yours.

—Mark 11:24

How is your prayer life? Have you been talking to God lately? What is the power of prayer? Those are not questions you are asked every day, are they! God means for our life to run on the power of prayer. So why is it hard to answer those questions for some?

Prayer fuels the engine of your heart and mind (yes, even more than coffee)! Prayer can be some people's lifeline, and for some, it is a mystery. How do we know if we are doing it right? Is it appropriate to ask for this or that? Is God answering any of our prayers?

Unfortunately for some, there is no simple answer. Fortunately for others, there are many ways to pray, and you can find what works for you! Prayer is real and personal. It can take seconds or hours. It is a conscious communication with God. You may kneel down and put your hands together and recite a memorized prayer, journal your prayers, talk out loud, keep it in your mind, pray with others, use beads, music—so many options.

Prayer is important in helping you to trust in God answering your prayers and patiently waiting for and accepting answers. It is important to lean on God and not on yourself. Here are some ways to become more comfortable with prayer:

1. Pick a time and a place to pray. You can pray anytime you want. However, the freedom to praying whenever you want sometimes leads to not praying at all. You might pray in

your car each morning or before bed at night. The Lord's Prayer is a very common prayer people say at night before sleep. Spontaneous prayer is still wonderful and should happen whenever it needs to happen.

2. Listen—don't just speak. On any given day, God may choose to move or "speak" in some unexpected way through his Spirit—bringing something to our mind, altering some circumstance, saying something through a friend., providing a rainbow in the sky—so let God speak.

3. Pray for your spiritual needs, not just physical, whether that be for ourselves or others.

4. Don't be afraid to stop and pray right now. So often, especially in the electronic age we live in, people ask for prayers more abundantly, which is wonderful. When you like that request or comment you are praying, are you praying right now? How many people say they will pray who actually forget to do it later? I challenge everyone to stop and pray before you post or like that request.

5. Identify your prayer groups—not real groups but a checklist, so to speak. Pray for yourself, your soul, then your spouse or partner, family, extended family, coworkers and neighbors, community, country, world, etc. Be willing to pray for those you might not necessarily agree with.

6. Pray for whatever you want! Seriously, nothing is too big, too small, too silly. Is praying for world peace too big to ask for? Maybe if one by one we add it to our list...

7. Be willing to ask and pray again. Persistence is okay. Be open to the answers you get, and acknowledge and pray for God's will to be done.

I encourage you to try some of these steps if you are new to prayer. A benefit to journaling your prayers—it is great to look back and see that God did answer your prayers even when you thought God wasn't listening.

Wednesday

For it is the Lord your God who goes with you, to fight
for you against your enemies, to give you victory.
—Deuteronomy 20:4

I find that scripture is very encouraging in so many ways! It is a reminder that nobody is alone in their battles. Whatever battle or enemy we are fighting, God is with us. Encouragement is the action of giving someone support or hope. We all need it, and we all should give it. It can provide the inspiration or strength someone needs during difficult times.

Encourage children! Sometimes the battle they are fighting seems minimal to us. Liking dressing themselves, going "potty," making their own lunch—it's really "big" to them at the time. Praise them, and encourage their little successes. Encourage them to keep trying! Surprise them with a little reward for good behavior you notice or just for continuing to try. Little bits of daily encouragement build up over time in growing their self-esteem.

Encourage people who are fighting an illness. Be there for them, say a prayer for them—even better, ask if there is something specific they would like you to pray for. Tell them you love them. Check in on them. Be there for them. Celebrate who they are despite the illness. That illness doesn't define them.

Encourage elderly people, caregivers, friends, coworkers—everyone. Recognize what people are doing, and support their dreams. Give someone hope when all seems to be going wrong. There is a silver lining they haven't seen yet! It's okay to be scared; it just means you're getting ready to be brave.

Life is full of bumps in the road, battles, wrong turns, and detours. Sometimes plans need to be adjusted, but it doesn't mean the goal does. Keep going in this journey, and take whatever life gives you. Learn what you can. Throw away the rest, and keep going. You're not alone!

> Take one day at a time. Today, after all, is the tomorrow you worried about yesterday. (Billy Graham)

Thursday

You were called to freedom, brothers and sisters; only
don't let this freedom be an opportunity to indulge your
selfish impulses, but serve each other through love.
—Galatians 5:13

Freedom is used to define so much in our lives—"land of the free,
home of the brave." What does it mean? How do we have that freedom? How do we share it peacefully?

Land of the free—we are *free* to do whatever we want. We
can practice the religion we want, have an education, job, money, a
home, etc.

Home of the brave—people were and are brave enough to come
and make America their home. We worry about the fighting in our
streets, the bad politics, the higher gas prices—yet people want to be
here. It is still better than where they came from.

If we are reading this scripture, why aren't we all choosing peace?
People want to be here to reap the rewards of our freedom, and why
wouldn't they? We should protect what is ours—our freedom; that
doesn't mean we don't share it. Our freedom gives us the right to love
each other, not to judge, to encourage everyone to have the successes
they want.

I hope to be "one nation under God" and be an example to
all, to spread love and not hate. Help people, find a way to love thy
neighbor. It starts with each one of us, and hopefully it is contagious
this Fourth of July.

God bless America!

Friday

He heals the brokenhearted, and binds up their wounds.

—Psalm 147:3

Comforting someone or sympathy is the understanding and reaction to the distress or need of another life form. Comforting someone who is grieving is not an easy task. While there is nothing you can do that can take their pain away, there are some ways that you can help them get through it. You can be there for them, comfort them.

Sometimes just sending a note or card helps provide comfort and peace of mind to someone who is mourning. However, finding the right words is tricky, and deciding what to write in a condolence card can be difficult. Sometimes being in person, giving a hug, holding a hand, and listening is what helps.

While we may not know what someone is going through, we do know that saying something is better than saying nothing at all. Just be yourself. Really witness their feelings. Listen to what they're going through. Support them. Help them if they want some help. Let them know you are there for them.

God helps us when we are down, and we should do the same for others. I'm sure many of us have encountered homeless people in our communities. Do you know their story? Have you ever asked how they got where they are? Do you give them money and say a prayer for them? A lot of those people have a story. We should hear their story and then help them move on and heal and then begin their journey.

Please reach out this month to those who are grieving, healing or just needing comfort. You don't have to do much—but a little gives hope.

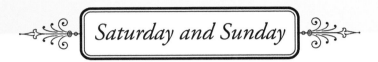
Saturday and Sunday

Above all, maintain constant love for one another,
for love covers a multitude of sins.

—1 Peter 4:8

To define unconditional love is to say that a person loves someone unselfishly, that he or she cares about the happiness of the other person and will do anything to help that person feel happiness without expecting anything in return. In giving the command to love one another, Jesus did something the world had never seen before—he created a group identified by one thing: *love*. There are many groups in the world, and they identify themselves in any number of ways—by skin color, by uniform, by shared interest, by alma mater, etc. One group has tattoos and piercings, another group eats meat, yet another group loves rainbows—the ways people categorize themselves are endless. But the church is unique. For the first and only time in history, Jesus created a group whose identifying factor is love. Skin color, native language—doesn't matter, no rules apply. Followers of Christ are identified by their love for each other.

We show love to others by forgiving, accepting and honoring them, by not judging them. When it comes to loving others, there are many, many ways to do so, but to start, pray for them. Praying for others daily is an impactful way of loving them unconditionally just as God calls us to do. We can also love unconditionally by accepting others, smiling at others (easy one), helping each other, making time for people, and be forgiving of others.

It is human nature for us to remove ourselves from situations that are uncomfortable like reaching out to those we don't know, forgiving those who have hurt us, being unselfish with those who are selfish. However, we are called to embrace the uncomfortable and really, truly love others.

Unconditional love is about how you act, not how you feel. It's about adapting to others' needs sometimes even when it is uncomfortable. It's about loving yourself and not judging yourself—important to practice this one. Try to do something each day to "practice" unconditional love. It can be letting someone through a door first, giving way to another car in a traffic jam, or telling someone you love them without expecting to hear it back in return. I promise—even though you don't want anything in return, you'll get a huge amount of pleasure from just giving unconditional love.

> Unconditional love is not based on the performance of the receiver, but on the character of the giver. (Jack Frost)

Ten Steps to Loving Unconditionally

Choose to Love Unconditionally

Let Go of Expectations

Accept the Other Person

Drop the Judgments

Speak Your Loved One's Love Language

Forgive Often

Love Yourself

Practice

Be Committed

Seek God

love

EMBRACING THE UNEXPECTED
MarenDee.com

Monday

> He said to them, "Come away to a deserted place all
> by yourselves and rest a while." For many were coming
> and going, and they had no leisure even to eat.
>
> —Mark 6: 31

Rest is important to your spiritual walk with the Lord, and many Christians today don't appreciate the value of rest or keeping the Sabbath day holy. Rest allows our mind, body, and soul to renew and start with even more strength and focus.

Life is busy and seems to get busier. How can we keep it all straight? Don't you long for a quiet night or day at home? Do you take vacation and really relax, or do you fill it with so much stuff you can't relax at all?

When you're sleeping well, it's much easier to manage stress. There are many benefits to getting enough rest in addition to managing stress. More rest helps boost your immune system and is good for your heart health. Adequate breaks also increase your mental energy and your creativity. More rest helps improve your short-term memory, and you actually are more productive at work when you allow yourself some rest.

With all these great benefits, how do we get more rest? God is an endless source of peace and strength, and he created a Sabbath day to allow ourselves a time to rest, relax, rejuvenate. It is very hard to take a day as a Sabbath day, and if you do, good job! If not, try to—it is worth it.

Summer is a good time of year to start including rest into your week. If you have to schedule rest, do it, and then keep the appointment! Take a few shorter breaks during a long day. Get more sleep. Allow yourself to walk in the park, hike, swim, bike, etc. It is okay and will help in the long run. Rest is just as important to your mind, body, and soul as exercise is. Press Pause for a bit. Stop at the rest area.

Tuesday

Whoever walks with the wise becomes wise, but
the companion of fools suffers harm.
—Proverbs 13:20

God knows our desire to be known and to be loved! He made us for companionship. This scripture is simply a reminder that we are the product of who we surround ourselves with. Friendship is one of the greatest gifts we can be given in our lifetime. Our friends can be the greatest source of love, healing, joy, and encouragement. Our friends can also be the greatest heartache, mistrust, and sadness.

Friendship is not a free gift. Long-lasting friendships require empathy, effort, and consistency. Friends require commitment, sacrifices, and loyalty. I believe the rewards of friendship are well worth the effort. I'm sure you can think of all kinds of friends you have had—childhood friends, school friends, college friends, sports friends. How many are still your friends? This number is normally much smaller for a number of reasons.

Friendship matters and is very important in our lives, and as we grow "up," we learn who our real friends are and who we should invest time in. Friendship gives us encouragement and support especially through challenging times. It also can help your self-esteem if your friend is reliable—someone you can count on. Choosing friends that are a positive influence over you is very important. Helps us make better decisions.

Sometimes life happens so fast; curve balls and wrong turns happen too. When you have hard times, who are the friends that are there for you? When things are good, who is there for you to celebrate? Don't spend a lot of energy worrying about why someone isn't there for you. Rather, spend positive energy making the friendships that count stronger. You deserve to be loved, supported, helped, believed in, and God reminds us of that.

Carole King, a great songwriter and singer, wrote a song about being a friend that is there for you no matter what. It was a song that nearly wrote itself, says King. It shows how we need a friend and how friendships can mean as much as family. It's about being there for those in need. If you would like to listen to the song, see the title here: "You've Got a Friend"

bit.ly/34mJyoh

Reach out to your friends today. Plan a coffee break. Stop by for a glass of wine. See a show together. Check on them. Be a good listener. If that's what they are needing, let them know you love them—it's a good day for that!

Other songs:

"I'll Be There For You" (The Rembrandts)

bit.ly/3q0NRhx

"Thank You For Being A Friend" (Andrew Gold)

bit.ly/3G2W3TX

"That's What Friends Are For" (Dionne Warwick)

bit.ly/3F1JJlC

But now ask the beasts, and they will teach you; And the
birds of the air, and they will tell you; Or speak to the earth,
and it will teach you; And the fish of the sea will explain
to you. Who among all these does not know That the
hand of the LORD has done this, In whose hand is the life
of every living thing, And the breath of all mankind?
—Job 12:7–10

Have you ever traveled somewhere and thought, *This is God's country*? Me too! It is an amazingly peaceful awe-inspiring feeling. Where is that for you? It used to be the mountains for me then the beach then the ocean then a hiking trail—no, wait, the river. God created an absolutely beautiful world full of peace!

It's important on this journey to take time to appreciate the world around you. We can't always take a big trip, but we can get outside. The value of this is immeasurable. It's important to remember what this world is like without all the "noise." No TV, no electronics, no news, no social media, etc., etc. Peaceful.

What can we do to preserve nature, maintain it, keep it? We can take care of it! Some ways to take care of nature, our environment: recycle, minimize electricity, have a compost, garden, pick up trash, carpool, bike, etc.

Share this beautiful creation (our world) with everyone! Explore the world, hike it, camp in it, dance in the rain, and really take it in. What does nature sound like, smell like, feel like, and of course, what are the colors of nature? There are many things you can do while enjoying nature: pray or meditate, sleep, dream, and most importantly—have hope!

> Study nature, love nature, stay close to nature. It will never fail you. (Frank Lloyd Wright)

Thursday

And he said to me, "Son of man, listen carefully and
take to heart all the words I speak to you."
—Ezekiel 3:10

Do you consciously set your heart to listening to God? Have you heard him? You must be ready to hear him. Be focused and not distracted. We need to shut off the "noise" around us to hear God. Prepare for a conversation with God as you would prepare to pray or meditate. Praying and reading the Bible are two ways to hear and see God's Word.

If you are willing to listen to God, are you willing to hear his message? Do you desire for his will to be done? These are important questions to answer when we think of listening to God. There are so many times in our lives that we ask God to do this or do that. We pray about a job, a relationship, for someone—and then we say, "God didn't answer."

God does answer. Sometimes it is not in the timeframe we are hoping, but he answers. Maybe God didn't say what you wanted to hear. When I think back in life and think about the "signs" or "answers" I missed, it is ridiculous. He answered, and if I would have listened, my journey would have sometimes been an easier path. They just were not the answers I was hoping for and looking for, but really they were. They were God's will, and I wasn't opening my heart to that.

Opening your heart to God's will will open your life up to wonderful things. You will receive the answers you are wanting to hear because they are God's answers. You will have a full life with abundant purpose, and most importantly, you will have confidence in knowing your life is part of the "master plan."

Regular conversation with God can transform your life! Consider identifying a place and time to meet with God every day. Why not start today?

Friday

To do righteousness and justice is more
acceptable to the Lord than sacrifice.

—Proverbs 21:3

To be a person of integrity is to be honest and have strong moral principles, moral uprightness. It means to be fair and truthful, do the right thing. We all hope that integrity is a quality people will see in us. If you have integrity, you are being true to yourself even when no one is looking.

This is one of those qualities that you should practice what you preach and lead by example daily. It's important to keep your promises always. Be a true friend, and don't start or be a part of gossip. If someone confides in you, keep that trust. Don't tell someone else.

Be honest in all situations. If someone gives you too much money back or undercharges you, be honest with them; that's how you would expect to be treated. Having integrity is living by your morals also. Be loyal to your partner, family, and friends.

Having integrity in the workplace or somewhere you serve is also important. Take responsibility for your actions. Don't let someone else take the blame for something that was wrong or not done. Work together as a team. Do your part on a project, and communicate with everyone.

Remember, understanding the actions caused by integrity starts with knowing what is important and holding fast to that idea even when it is not convenient or to your benefit.

> Perhaps the surest test of an individual's integrity is his refusal to do or say anything that would damage his self-respect. (Thomas S. Monson)

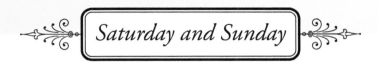

Saturday and Sunday

Then they said to him, "Inquire of God that we may know whether the mission we are undertaking will succeed." The priest replied, "Go in peace. The mission you are on is under the eye of the Lord."
—Judges 18:5–6

How's your journey going? Do you ever wonder if you're on the right path?

You are! God knows the journey, the mission you are on. Have faith. You may have some setbacks, but you are still not alone.

What is the next journey you are going on this summer? Choosing *peace*? What's your next step to make it happen? Have you been praying for it? Staying in touch with people? Serving those around you? Listening to God or having a talk with him?

Take some time this weekend to make a mental checklist of what the next week or two looks like for you. What's your path, and how do you make sure you have things that are important—comfort, joy, and love? Pack lightly!

Bring comfy shoes, favorite T-shirt, and feel comfort. Bring yourself some good music—something that makes you want to sing out loud, something that makes you happy. Maybe a meditation tape or podcast to better your life and those around you.

Whatever your journey you are embarking on, pack light! Simple is better. Really focus on what you are trying to accomplish. God knows your mission!

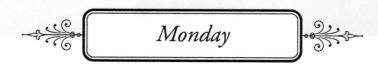

Monday

Don't hesitate to be enthusiastic—be on fire
in the Spirit as you serve the Lord!

—Romans 12:11

Everything in this world seeks to bring us down, but we have to be determined to keep going when the times are hard. God will guide us in life and help us through everything. Believe, and let go of doubt, stress, and fear by trusting with everything you have!

Focusing on the end goal is keeping your determination. Try to block out the negative and troubling things going on. Those things are hard, and they are there. Don't feed them any more energy than they already have. God will always work in your life and do the things you can't. He will carry you when you think you're all alone.

Let's get excited about serving the Lord and choosing peace! Here are five steps to keep our determination in check:

1. Manage your time. No matter how hard you try, if you don't know how to manage your time, then success is a far off thing for you. Set a time limit for certain tasks, have a schedule, stick to it.
2. Make a to-do list. Yes, this takes time, but it will save time in the long run. If you stick to your list, it will help you stay focused on the task at hand.
3. Make time to reflect on your day. What did you achieve? Was it a tough day—but you got through it? Pray about this.

4. Believe in yourself! You are worthy of great things. You deserve success in whatever it is you are striving for.
5. Don't believe that stress is necessary. It is *not*. Stress accomplishes nothing. Excitement at the prospect is what helps. Stress will take away steps 1–4 if you let it.

Sometimes the hardest things bring the greatest rewards, and that really is true. We learn from so much that happens in our world and in our lives. So set your sight on this and try this week to do these five steps and see where your heart is by Friday evening. I believe it will be in faith with God and feeling wonderful about your journey.

> You've got to get up every morning with determination if you're going to go to bed with satisfaction. (George Horace Lorimer)

Tuesday

I have said these things to you so that my joy may
be in you, and that your joy may be complete.

—John 15:11

Yes, be happy! We just naturally, instinctively want to be happy, so we pursue happiness, just as we always have; and if we follow God, we will find happiness. There are some who think that God doesn't want us to be happy. They are under the impression that things that bring joy to our hearts are not good, and the "science of happiness" tells us happiness is a choice. Still struggling with how to be happy?

There are reasons we may not think—or that we may take for granted:

- There are people who love you unconditionally, and they want to see you happy. *Choose* happiness for the people who love you.
- Life can change at a moment's notice. *Choose* happiness today, and enjoy every single moment you have.
- Happy people are more productive. *Choose* happiness, and be more likely to accomplish your goals.
- The world needs more happy people. Good triumphs over evil, and there is a lot of bad going on right now. *Choose* happiness.
- You are alive. You're tired, sick, unhappy, but you can be grateful that you are alive, and you can be with the people you love most. *Choose* to live.

- Surveys say happy people have better relationships, whether that is at work or with family and friends. *Choose* togetherness.
- Being happy is good for you! It lowers stress, helps your self-esteem, people tend to exercise more, it is directly correlated to being healthy. *Choose* health.

Feel happiness now, spread joy, and increase peace—don't wait 'til tomorrow.

Wednesday

Do not let any unwholesome talk come out of your mouths,
but only what is helpful for building others up according
to their needs, that it may benefit those who listen.
—Ephesians 4:29

Do you ever pay attention to how much judging really goes on around us on a daily basis? How often do we hear comments about people, this, that or the other—that aren't necessary? Are you making them yourself? Honestly, we all do it, and for what? Take a piece of paper and for one day keep track of what you hear, what you say, the activity going on around you. We are a community of people saying it is not our place to judge (God does that), yet we probably do it more than we are aware of.

What benefit comes from judging others? Does it make someone feel better about themselves, take attention away from themselves, or just give someone power to be hurtful, bossy, etc.? When we are aware of it, it happens less. This judging others and things has to end to bring peace to our lives on all levels.

Sometimes people judge things by the cost: material objects, price for a night's stay—must be better if it costs more or the opposite, must be too fancy because it costs more. Sometimes people are judged by cleanliness of other things. They assume someone is poor, doesn't care, homeless if they are "unclean," and maybe they are—but why judge them? Why not find out what their story is?

We tend to comment, not knowing anything about someone. We shouldn't compare people to ourselves or to anyone else. After all, we are all uniquely created. We shouldn't be just like anyone else.

We should honor and celebrate the differences around us. We should take note of them and communicate to learn more about each other, about our community, and use useful, uplifting comments.

A View from a Train Window

A twenty-four-year-old man is looking out of a train's window and shouting loudly, ""Dad, look, the trees are going behind!"

His father smiled and noticed a young couple sitting nearby who were observing the twenty-four-year-old's childish behavior with pity.

Suddenly, the young man again exclaimed, ""Dad, look, the clouds are running with us!"

The couple couldn't resist and said to the old man: "Why don't you take your son to a good doctor?"

"The old man smiled and said, "I did, and we are just coming from the hospital. My son was blind from birth. He just got his eyes today."

Every single person on the planet has a story. Don't judge people before you truly know them. The truth might surprise you.

Thursday

A person's pride will bring humiliation, but one
who is lowly in spirit will obtain honor.

—Proverbs 29:23

Honor is worth so much. Respect comes from honor. How do we differentiate between what we know and what we know is right? Are we living the way our moms and dads would want? Or how Jesus would? Or ourselves?

It's hard to differentiate what is right and what is wanted. If you are called a person of honor, you are respected. If someone honors you, they recognize and award you for being your true self, for your achievements and your compassion. With honor, there is righteousness and integrity. That is why people always associate character with honorable conduct. This is to inspire the world that honor is as important as life.

Live with truth, integrity, faith, and love. These characteristics encompass what God wants from us. What can we do to live a life of honor? Walk in Jesus's footsteps. Help people. Believe in them. Love them. Live how you think God would want you to live. Honor other people. Respect them.

Living by example is a great way to teach integrity to children and to those around us. Fight the urge to be self-serving. Try to put others first. Respect your parents, your elders. They really do know a thing or two. Honor God by sharing his love for everyone by doing just that!

Friday

But grow in the grace and knowledge of our Lord and Savior
Jesus Christ. To him be glory both now and forever! Amen.
—2 Peter 3:18

When we become Christians, we enter into a relationship with God,
Jesus, and the Holy Spirit that will cause us to grow. How do we grow
up? Is there a difference between growing as "humans" and growing
as "children of God"? Where does spiritual growth tie into this all?

I'm sure there are basic things we need to grow up or mature:

- We need to nourish our bodies.
- We need to protect ourselves.
- We need to breathe and sleep.
- We need to be responsible.
- We need to love.

So how can we apply these to growing as children of God?

- We can nourish ourselves with information. Scripture has a
  lot of that; read an affirmation daily.
- We need to make good choices to protect ourselves, follow
  the commandments.
- We need to pray or meditate.
- We need to take care of others, serve those who need to be
  served.
- We need to love our families, love our neighbors, surround
  ourselves with people who care.

Growth is so much more than becoming an adult. As an adult, I have grown more than I ever did as a child. Experiencing life is a large part of growing up. It's important to expose yourself to the world around you and learn from it. It's important to be selfless and think outside your "box." I grew up very oblivious to the world around me, which was good when I was younger. I know now the world around me that I lived in was very hard. A lot of bad things happened in it. I love my version of the world I grew up in—my la-la land. It helped me to not be cynical and negative, not hold grudges, not blame others. It helped me survive and have the positive energy to want to choose *peace*!

Hopefully, your experiences as you grow help you grow in God's image.

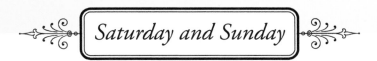

Saturday and Sunday

The Lord said, "If as one people speaking the same
language they have begun to do this, then nothing
they plan to do will be impossible for them."
—Genesis 11:6

Imagination is the action of forming new ideas or images or concepts
of external objects not present to the senses. It is the ability of the
mind to be creative or resourceful. Imagination is what allows us to
dream and to hope. Do you ever get so caught up in your routine
that you don't dream anymore? Or so worried about what something
will cost, how it will get done, where you will find the time? We
must allow ourselves to think outside the box to move forward, and
it is faith that supports us while we do this. We have to keep creating opportunities to be creative not only for ourselves but for our
children. Dreaming has to continue to keep growing and moving
forward.

Imagination is a gift from above. It is imagination that gives us
the power to see a slum as a city with paved streets. It is imagination
that allows us to see our world as it is meant to be, and it is prayer
that unlocks the power of imagination.

Do you think we would ever have landed on the moon if someone hadn't imagined what it would be like? Someone had to imagine
being an astronaut, a teacher, a pilot. Everyone pretends when they
are growing up, and that creativity gives power to ideas and desires.
Someone had to dream of it and pray about the possibilities. If we are
praying and listening to God, nothing is impossible!

Monday

Praise the LORD who has given his people
peace, as he promised he would.

—1 Kings 8:56

Focus your mind and heart on God, and let your praise go up. God is worthy of our praise. We have so much to praise God for. There's great power in giving honor to him. Many of you live that truth out every single day of your lives. Some of us give praise when we feel a miracle has occurred or a prayer has been answered. Yet reality is that way too often—daily struggles or constant life demands can crowd out our praise to God.

Sometimes it is really hard to offer praise. We may not feel like it; we're struggling with things in life or have suffered through something, and we may just be mad and feel God wasn't there when we needed help. Praise can make a lasting difference. You may find when you decide to regularly praise God that your struggles and suffering were not endured alone and are easier.

There's power in our acknowledgement that God is worthy of our worship and praise. Whether you sing or pray, feel like it or not doesn't matter. What does matter is that your heart is in it—wholly. Praise can help us get our focus back on God and not on ourselves. Praise will help us acknowledge our need for God. God is in control. It also helps us stay positive, focus on all the blessings in our lives.

Praise invites God's presence, and we are strengthened by the peace and joy of God. God changes our hearts and helps work through us. Miracles happen in our lives when we allow God in our hearts. The Spirit urges us onward, calling us closer.

Pray for ways to praise, and you will find there is no right way except with your heart. Let God hear your praise and watch yourself blossom. Let go of the worry and stress of everything.

Check out this song title to listen to a beautiful song about praising God! "10,000 Reasons" (Bless the Lord), sung here by Matt Redman: bit.ly/3eXdFon.

Tuesday

> And this is love: that we walk in obedience to his
> commands. As you have heard from the beginning,
> his command is that you walk in love.
>
> —2 John 1:6

The biblical word for *obey* comes from the Greek "hupakou," which means "to listen attentively; to heed or conform to a command or authority." It gives you the idea of actively following a command, and to walk in love doesn't sound like it should be that hard, right?

Most of us don't like rules. We don't like being told what to do, when to do it, how often—especially as adults. We like to be independent and make our own decisions. We know what is best, right? Obedience isn't just for kids though. We don't really have any idea what is best sometimes, and we make mistake after mistake—and God gives us grace and love.

So today, let's try to "walk in love." Consciously try today to do just that. Instead of being angry about morning traffic, enjoy the time for you: pray, sing out loud, smile, let that car in that's been waiting to pull out. Long line for coffee? Buy someone else a cup while you're there. Drive-through taking forever? Smile and think how frustrated the employee who is short staffed feels. Grab a cold water for your postal person—it's hot out there. There are many opportunities to show God's love to people if we just open our eyes to what is happening all around us.

Walking in obedience will actually help you feel relief from stress, allow yourself to focus on other things, other people, and let go of all the pressure you put on yourself. It is also a true sign of your love for God, which mirrors God's love for you!

Wednesday

He will once again fill your mouth with laughter
and your lips with shouts of joy.

—Job 8:21

Joy is a feeling of great pleasure and happiness. Christian joy is a good feeling in the soul produced by the Holy Spirit as it causes us to see the beauty of Christ in the Word and in the world. What are you doing in the world that is causing you joy? What are you doing to feel happy?

With all the suffering and pain in the world, it is sometimes hard to feel joyful or happy, but it is a necessity in life. To choose good things, we need positive energy helping us along the way. We need to let go of some worries and enjoy this life God gave us. Easier said than done.

Here are four things to do to find joy that makes sense:

1. Do things that you know make you happy! Listen to the eighties music that makes you want to sing and dance. Wear bright colors. Act like a kid. Make time for fun!

2. Express gratitude: "Thank you" isn't so tough. Showing appreciation is important in your own feelings. Don't take things for granted.

3. Is your hobby your passion? If not, change it! Do something that you are passionate about and gives you purpose. Figure out what inspires you, and do it; it actually has amazing effects on your brain.

4. Invest in good relationships; they are what will help you maintain your joy. Make time for people who make time for you. It's okay to "prune" your social circle and get rid of the "bad apples." Negative energy is not going to bring you joy.

For more examples and links to other ways to make those four things happen, check out "This Is How to Find Joy: Four Simple Secrets to the Good Life"

bit.ly/31wKMMI

Let's put ourselves out there and do something good for someone else. Do something for yourself—and feel what happens. This is joy, and once you feel it, you will know hope, peace, patience, kindness, goodness, faithfulness, gentleness, and self-control. And it is in those feelings that you will come to know God.

Thursday

But the plans of the LORD stand firm forever, the
purposes of his heart through all generations.
—Psalm 33:11

Purpose can guide life decisions, influence behavior, shape goals, offer a sense of direction, and create meaning. For some people, purpose is connected to vocation—meaningful, satisfying work. For others, their purpose lies in their responsibilities to their family or friends. Do you know what your purpose is? If you do, are you living each day to the fullest with the intent on fulfilling your purpose? If you don't, how do you know?

I was in a car accident in my early twenties. Pretty bad—car was totaled, and I was very protected by God that day. My doctor ran numerous x-rays and tests because he couldn't believe I wasn't more seriously hurt, let alone I survived. He told me, "You must not have done what you were sent here for because God could have taken you in that accident." I know many, many people who have been in terrible accidents, have had to fight horrible diseases, and they are here—to serve God's purpose is the only explanation that makes sense.

I think believing that we have a purpose is more important than sometimes knowing what it is. Knowing you have purpose in life helps you live life with integrity. People who know their purpose in life know who they are, what they are, and why they are; and when you know yourself, it becomes easier to live a life that's true to your core values. Some of us hold many jobs before we fill the role we were meant to fill. Some people feel they don't know their purpose; however, the people around them tell the story of their purpose.

There are many benefits to living your purpose like staying focused. If you know your purpose, you can focus on doing the things that help you fulfill it. It also helps you be passionate about something. Whether it is a childhood dream or a new lifestyle, the passion will help you achieve it and stick to it. A person who knows their purpose tends to make a greater impact through their work, which encourages a feeling of gratification.

Living a purpose-driven life can really make life fun. Even the most boring things can become creative and beautiful! It helps some people find a flow. People tend to allow life to happen and accept the challenges along the way and battle against their fears but not fight the flow of life.

When you commit to living your life with a purpose, amazing things can happen.

I encourage you today to think about your purpose or lack of knowing your purpose and figure out what you do know. I couldn't tell you exactly what my purpose is, but I do know that choosing *peace* is part of it!

Friday

Let us not become weary in doing good, for at the proper
time we will reap a harvest if we do not give up.
—Galatians 6:9

News, social media, anger, violence—all these things can be very discouraging. Discouragement and disappointment are normal emotions we all experience, but it's important to make sure those emotions don't get the best of us. It's important to remember that God is with you through all of it and will carry you through.

It's so easy to get disappointed in how something turns out or to feel misunderstood. We get frustrated with a lack of motivation or procrastination that is affecting our plans. We feel we are not living up to someone else's expectations. That disappointment can lead to discouragement, and we have to know things are happening for a reason. Sometimes this bad or disappointing thing will lead to a bigger, better thing. Even the strongest people get discouraged.

What can we do to help when we find someone (or ourselves) feeling discouraged? We really have to be honest. Don't pretend to be positive if you aren't feeling it. Don't say everything is okay if it really isn't. Acknowledging the disappointment is a great step in addressing it. Pay attention to the way you are thinking about things. Are you having a negative thought for everything? Change it up, find a couple of scriptures that remind you that God has a plan: Jeremiah 29:11 or Romans 8:28 or Philippians 4:13.

Be thankful for God's will. Gratitude is a powerful anecdote for discouragement. Life is hard, and bad things happen, but don't dwell on those things. Find a silver lining. Find a purpose for the discouragement you are feeling, and you will start to see things differently.

Discouragement is a temptation—you have to fight it. Don't let it take over *you*. Take comfort in your faith, and gain encouragement. Hold your head up, and don't worry about things that are out of our control; instead, focus on what you can control—your faith in God and this journey.

> You have been assigned this mountain to show others it can be moved.

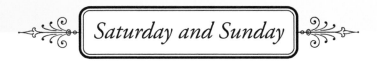

Saturday and Sunday

Fight the good fight of the faith. Take hold of the eternal
life to which you were called when you made your good
confession in the presence of many witnesses.
—2 Timothy 4:7

Adventure is defined as "an unusual and exciting, typically hazard-ous experience or activity." This is exactly what many biblical figures underwent as they were called upon to go into the unknown in the work of God. Our life can be an adventure in the service of righteous-ness, facing the adversity and evils of the world. Find inspiration to live adventurously from Scripture and the stories on your journey.

When your heart is set upon Christ, the Christian life is far from boring. It's filled with adventure and many exciting moments. It is a lifelong journey in which you are being molded into the image of God. When you spend time in the presence of the Lord, you will become bolder, and you will be more effective when God uses you around your community. Prayer, meditation, devotions all can lead us to adventurous situations.

Our youth are serving on a mission trip that will be an adven-ture. They will encounter people and situations that are different sometimes than their own, yet they are walking the path God is lead-ing them, and they will have stories to tell. People serve at Harvester's each month, and they do a lot of work to help a lot of people who need food. Each month is a new adventure! Some people volunteer to teach Sunday school of different age groups, and that is truly an adventure. The stories and insight gained from the innocent, loving minds of children is immeasurable.

The common thread here is in each example. Someone is witnessing for a Christian, love-filled presence, and all are experiencing different adventures. I encourage you to spend time with someone who is doing one of those things and listen. If you find yourself thinking your life is a little boring compared to theirs, then get out there and seek out adventure in the name of Christ.

Here are just a few ways you can create some adventure in your life:

- Volunteer (teach Sunday school, lead a small group)
- Serve (help in a food pantry or clothes closet, go on a mission trip)
- Listen (talk to someone in need, and hear their story)
- Communicate (reach out to people you haven't talked to in a long time, appreciate someone, show gratitude)

You will touch so many lives and enhance yours. What are you waiting for?

Monday

Trust in the Lord forever, for in the Lord
God[a] you have an everlasting rock.

—Isaiah 26:4

When trials hit our lives or when it seems everything around us is falling apart, we as Christians need daily reminders to be stable. Having the stability as a follower of Christ proclaims a lot to an unstable and sinful world. On the flip side, when we are unstable, we are forgetting who is on the throne. When we are stable, we have the strength to stand and endure some of the trials around us.

If God, who is the creator of everything, can actually have a relationship with us because of what Jesus did for us, then surely we can find stability in him. He is the reason we can be stable. He is the One who is at work at all times, in all circumstances, and never becomes unstable.

Anxious of your future?

Thinking our country is headed in the wrong direction?

Worried about your kids or your family?

Struggling in your own personal relationships with others?

Obsessed with the balance of your bank account?

Whatever it is in your life that is leading you to think you are unstable, it is not bigger than God. While there are difficult circumstances to go through, you can trust in the One who is stable to lead you through it. The more we can look up to God and not look to ourselves, the more stable we will become.

So, how do we do that? How do we create and practice more stability in our lives? Meditating is a great way to focus and center yourself. Try to take the focus off the instability around us. This will retrain your brain to make more conscious choices for your happiness by clearing the clutter. You could exercise or try yoga.

A great way to find stability is to unplug from technology. Do you have thirty minutes a day you can do that? How about your evenings? How much time do you spend checking out all the chaos that happened today? Put it down, turn it off. Detoxing your mind away from the push-and-pull energy of constant stimulation is healthy in all ways. Try to increase the amount of time each day. You will find it gets easier to have positive thoughts when you have a clear mind.

Surround yourself with positive people! Your family and your friends, people who can help create calm. Today, choose stability instead of turmoil. I promise that you will feel more grounded and at home in your heart. Remember, we are happiest when we are peaceful.

Tuesday

Cast all your anxiety on him, because he cares for you.
—1 Peter 5:7

Struggles come in all shapes and sizes—fears, addictions, persecution, and worries can all seem to take over our thoughts. We will often bring this struggle upon ourselves by not seeking the Lord with choices and decisions in our life. It is often a repeating cycle of one bad choice leading to another. God tells us that we will face trials but that we should not lose hope! Be encouraged because you do have choices, and you are not alone.

There are many stories of struggling before becoming successful. Probably some people you have heard of are:

- *J. K. Rowling*: Rowling may be rolling in a lot of *Harry Potter* dough today, but before she published the series of novels, she was nearly penniless, severely depressed, divorced, trying to raise a child on her own while attending school and writing a novel. Rowling went from depending on welfare to survive to being one of the richest women in the world in a span of only five years through her hard work and determination.
- *Ludwig Van Beethoven*: In his formative years, young Beethoven was incredibly awkward on the violin and was often so busy working on his own compositions that he neglected to practice. Despite his love of composing, his teachers felt he was hopeless at it and would never succeed with the violin or in composing. Beethoven kept plugging

along, however, and composed some of the best-loved symphonies of all time—five of them while he was completely deaf.

- *Michael Jordan*: Most people wouldn't believe that a man often lauded as the best basketball player of all time was actually cut from his high school basketball team. Luckily, Jordan didn't let this setback stop him from playing the game, and he has stated, "I have missed more than nine thousand shots in my career. I have lost almost three hundred games. On twenty-six occasions, I have been entrusted to take the game winning shot, and I missed. I have failed over and over and over again in my life—and that is why I succeed."

- *Walt Disney*: Today Disney rakes in billions from merchandise, movies, and theme parks around the world, but Walt Disney himself had a bit of a rough start. He was fired by a newspaper editor because "he lacked imagination and had no good ideas." After that, Disney started a number of businesses that didn't last too long and ended with bankruptcy and failure. He kept plugging along, however, and eventually found a recipe for success that worked.

When you think of some of the above success stories, think of what we wouldn't have if they had given up! You never know what is in store for you—keep on going. Really try to trust God, follow his path, and try to not take the long way around every time. There are things we learn from our struggles. We get stronger from these struggles.

Here is a great list I felt connected pretty well with overcoming struggles, a "what can I do" list for myself. I encourage you to check it out too! Twenty Ways to Overcome Life Struggles by Live Bold and Bloom.

bit.ly/3JNygtD

Wednesday

In the same way, let your light shine before people, so they can see
the good things you do and praise your Father who is in heaven.
—Matthew 5:16

Does the thought of witnessing to others about your faith excite you
or stress you out? Many people think of sharing their faith as either
a death sentence or a commandment enforced by knocking on doors
and throwing Bibles. Fortunately, this is not true! We serve a loving
God who doesn't want us to condemn each other. You can spread
God's love and joy by approaching witnessing with the right attitude
and state of mind.

Witnessing is all in how you live your life. We are not com-
manded to share our faith yet, to encourage each other, be there for
each other. Share with those around you with your heart. Send someone a card, or take time to call someone. Don't shy away from someone who is going through a hard time. God gives us these opportunities to bring comfort to people.

Witnessing may be living by example—sometimes even if you
are the only one. It also is sharing our struggles. Share your struggles
with people you trust. Overcome the fear—it is empowering! And let
people try to be there with you and for you. Be open to what God is
laying before you on this journey. Share your successes, how God has
helped you, loved you. Don't be offended if someone questions your
story. Look at it as them seeking their answers.

Witnessing is a great responsibility and opportunity to share
your love of Christ. Remember that we all have our story, our own
journey, but also, God is with each of us on that journey. Sometimes

opportunities just arise, and it is God working in both situations to create unity in the spirit of love. It is helping each other even when we don't really know it is happening.

A witness is one who sees or observes an event, so sharing your experiences are important, and sharing how God has worked in your life is the other part of it.

Witnessing is purely you—speaking your truth from your heart.

Thursday

If possible, to the best of your ability, live at peace with all people.
—Romans 12:18

Choosing *peace*—what a journey! So many factors into how that happens—love, trust, strength, protection, faith, joy—it happens, this journey, when we begin searching for answers differently than we did before. We slow down and really start to think about things. We turn inward. When this happens, we begin the journey.

The spiritual journey, the journey to wisdom, the journey to peace and happiness, the path of awakening or liberation, whatever you want to call it, it's the same—it's the path we begin on when we break the cycle of consumption and unhealthy methods of filling the "void" and begin looking within.

I hope if you are reading this, you are experiencing this on some level and feeling very proud! Whether you are far along the path or just beginning, it's a good place to be; and while this journey may look different from person to person, it's the same goal for all of us—it's the gradual process of peeling back the layers of yourself to find a progressively greater level of peace (and much joy) through understanding yourself and your place in the world.

Take a look at where you are looking for peace: yourself, your family and home, your community, the world—all of those. Please take a look at the following "tips," and really make a note of where you are or what you can do to work on each one of these. I feel an increased awareness of how I am looking at this world as I walk this journey and can always use some fine-tuning.

- Like/Love yourself. Don't compare yourself to others.
- Receive God's forgiveness.
- Accept other people just the way they are.
- Remember to let God have control of your life (this one is tough for me).
- Watch your tongue—speak kindly of others.
- Stay fearless. Don't give up. Be tough.
- Be gracious. Daily think of the little things that add to the big things, and be thankful for them.
- Seek to love, not control others.
- Live in joy. It's good to be happy and find laughter.
- Think peace. Be peace. Be the change you wish to see in the world.

Life is all about balance. Being productive and achieving success is one-half of the equation, but the other half is finding peace in your life!

Friday

Then people will come from east and west, from north
and south, and will eat in the kingdom of God.
—Luke 13:29

Getting away is a natural desire, a normal occurrence. People want
to leave behind, even temporarily, the routine that is day to day. It's
important to go and experience other places, other cultures, and
other people; and when we do travel, it's important to try and be a
part of where we visit.

Jesus traveled often. He didn't stay in one location. He went
with his family to a festival annually for three years to celebrate
Passover. They traveled to Jerusalem and then stayed for a seven-day
Unleavened Bread Festival.

He went to meet people, see other places, learn about geogra-
phy, and meet other worshippers of various other religions. He went
to the temple, went to the Jordan River, many journeys to meet people, heal people, spread God's love.

There are things you can do while traveling to be a part of their
community. Ask around for the best local places to dine (you'll most
likely get the best food and meet local people); take a tour if there
is one available (you'll learn history of the place, and often the tour
guide has lived "there" their entire life); go to church wherever you
are visiting (do they worship like you do, love God like you do?).

Immerse yourself in the natural environment of where you visit.
Be a part of it, ask questions, be kind, be gracious, and smile. I hope
you will find there is kindness everywhere, concerns everywhere, and

a common goal of peace everywhere; and in return, welcome visitors to your community. Kindness and good hospitality is a reciprocal act.

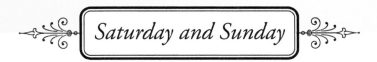

Saturday and Sunday

Speaking to one another with psalms, hymns, and songs from the Spirit. Sing and make music from your heart to the Lord.
—Ephesians 5:19

Music is holy. Rejoice in the sound! God created us to be instruments with the ability to sing and make music. Music is an important part of worship and praise to God. Our church had two services to provide different music to different people: we had a soloist, choir, and organist at one and a worship band for the other. Some people like traditional hymns; some like more contemporary gospel and Christian music.

Some people wonder if Christians can listen to rap, country, rock, pop, R and B, etc. Of course! Music is so powerful and can have an extremely big effect on how you live your life. It's important to try and monitor the type of music being listened to. All genres can have positive music. There are negative too, and those are not recommended. Choose your music wisely!

Music is a great way to encourage family communications, turn off the TV, and crank some tunes! Listen to and respect each other's music. Dance and sing and have fun together. I love all different types of music. The genre varies, depending on the song, what is happening in my life and what speaks to me. Music has helped me figure a lot of things out and also helped me relax and have fun.

Music to me is a gateway to the soul. When you sing, meditate, or just get into the groove of a song and also think about Christ, your soul intertwines itself with the music, and you might just get motivated to get out there and tell people God loves them! Music is an awesome thing!!

Monday

Love is patient; love is kind; love is not envious or
boastful or arrogant or rude. It does not insist on its own
way; it is not irritable or resentful; it does not rejoice in
wrongdoing, but rejoices in the truth. It bears all things,
believes all things, hopes all things, endures all things.
—1 Corinthians 13:4–7

Love is a variety of feelings, emotions, and attitudes. It is an intense feeling of deep affection. Love can also be described as the breath of the Holy Spirit. Love is what connects divine creation to the realities of life. Wow! Sounds so powerful, and it truly is an all-encompassing feeling.

How do we live unconditionally? How do we know God loves us? There are things that show us he does. We woke up this morning! That shows you God's plans for you are not over. Go out and spread kindness, love, and his word.

People are brought into your life continuously—sometimes for a lifetime, sometimes for a minute, always for a reason. We don't meet people on accident, and God challenges us! Life isn't easy. I believe God knows our plan, and no matter what challenges arise, good will come of it.

God loves you! Believe it, live it, and experience it all. It is not easy. There are so many things that make us question God's love for us. However, it is there and always will be there! Allow yourself to feel love, and pray about it. It is divinely for you!!!

Tuesday

Whether you turn to the right or turn to the left, your ears will hear a voice behind you, saying, "This is the way; walk in it."
—Isaiah 30:21

The Bible is a tremendous source for those seeking guidance in their life. From the wisdom and knowledge of Scripture, we can make improved decisions and become better people as we navigate the complexity of the world. Scripture will give you the clarity you are looking for—if you read it, if you believe it.

Do you ever just wish God would give you a sign, something to help you navigate through negative thoughts, relationships, jobs, maybe a major purchase, etc.? Or maybe you've heard someone say, "I keep waiting for a sign." We're all looking for clarity, and it's great to be looking to God for it. However, are we open to it? Are we ready for the sign he gives us or keeps giving us?

If you are lacking clarity, you probably find yourself changing your mind a lot, questioning yourself, and feeling overwhelmed. You might also be tired, unorganized, even distracted. So you need some clarity in your life, some focus.

Do you know where you're wanting clarity or answers in your life? Because if you are changing your mind all the time, the answers you are getting may be for what you wanted before. Ask yourself a couple of questions to put things in perspective:

What do you *have* clarity in? And how does that affect your feelings?

What is something you *don't* have clarity in? And how is that making you feel?

Try making a list of what you need to figure out. Could be one thing; it could be many. Then try to look at what you can do to change your mindset on one of the things on your list. Then pray about that, and pray to be open to what God leads you to. Sometimes we get so focused on the answer we want that we miss the answer altogether, and we stay unhappy, unorganized, etc.

Having clarity will, no matter what, bring good to your life. It opens doors, closes doors, fills our hearts, brings us to things we never dreamed of, and you will feel better about yourself, your life, and about your relationship with God.

Wednesday

For the grace of God has been revealed,
bringing salvation to all people.

—Titus 2:11

Grace is seen as enabling power and spiritual healing offered through the mercy and love of Jesus Christ. Some see grace as getting what we don't deserve. It is the love of God shown to the unlovely, peace given to the restless.

How do we live in grace? Jesus showed grace in many ways. We can implement what he did in our own lives each day. Here are some ways Jesus showed grace:

1. He showed compassion to everyone
2. He forgave his enemies.
3. He helped those that were labeled "outcasts." Have you ever felt like an outcast?
4. He spoke the truth. Jesus knew what each person needed to hear and gave them the truth.
5. He spoke truth in love and showed us that grace is reasonable.
6. He was patient. He did things in God's time whether he agreed or not.
7. He sacrificed and endured great pain even when it cost him.
8. Jesus gave because he loved.

Put these practices into your life. Give grace to those you might think don't deserve it. Help people without judgment. Use kind words. Smile at people. Assume the best rather than the worst. Grace is powerful and fills your life with gratitude and peace. Use it, and pass it on.

Thursday

The attitude that comes from selfishness leads to death, but the attitude that comes from the Spirit leads to life and peace.!
—Romans 8:6

The definition of *spirituality* is "the quality of being concerned with the human spirit or soul as opposed to material or physical things." In general, it includes a sense of connection to something bigger than ourselves, and it typically involves a search for meaning in life. As such, it is a universal human experience—something that touches us all in different ways.

Spirituality can mean different things to different people, something different depending on what religion we practice too. Some of us identify or look at our spirituality as prayer and meditation. Maybe it is yoga and breathing; for some, being in the environment is spiritual. I personally feel if I make time to meditate, I touch base with my spiritual side. I take time to focus on "nothing" around me. I get in touch with the soul that drives my journey.

There are many different things you can do at church for spiritual growth. You can read your Bible or join a small group or Bible study, read devotionals, or intentionally pray every day. Go to church, get baptized. Deciding to follow Jesus helps in spiritual growth. Serve others, and give your time, your money (any way you give of yourself).

How can we practice spirituality in our own lives, not just at church, you may wonder?

"Five Ways to Put Spirituality in Practice" is a great little resource (bit.ly/3qXyuWf). You will see that the list is very similar to the things you can do at church. Spirituality is part of each person's path, part of your journey.

It may be part of your goal for self-development, part of your relationship with God. Whatever it is—it is yours to nurture and grow.

> We are not human beings having a spiritual experience. We are spiritual beings having a human experience. (Pierre Teilhard de Chardin)

Friday

Give, and it will be given to you. A good measure, pressed down,
shaken together and running over, will be poured into your lap.
For with the measure you use, it will be measured to you.

—Luke 6:38

The lesson of having open hands and sharing with others is not just a lesson for kids! As adults, God calls us to share with those in need and to live a generous life. Sharing does not only bless those we give to, but it blesses us as well! You will never know a full and joyful life until you are able to give out of generosity and share what God has given you.

There are so many ways to share! We often think of sharing with the needy and poor, which is great. We also can share our ideas, a ride, some cookies, our love, our experiences—all have value to someone else. How often do you "share" a random act of kindness? Have you noticed people performing random acts of kindness? Can you make a list of different things you can do?

Sharing ourselves unselfishly is a gift not only to others but to ourselves! The feelings you get are numerous: proud, happy, joyous, unselfish, loving, excited, caring, etc., and think about when others are kind to you—someone holds the door for you, smiles, pays for your coffee in the drive-through—what a great start to your day. Oftentimes that kindness can change your outlook for the day or even become contagious so that you want to pay it forward. I challenge you to start a pattern of doing random acts of kindness. Here is a list to get you started!

Fifty-One Random Acts of Kindness Ideas
These are from the "Local Adventurer"
website: bit.ly/3EVR3PO

Send someone a handwritten letter or postcard.

Bring someone a souvenir.

Cook someone a meal.

Bake someone treats.

Put your phone away (especially if you're on it a lot).

Do someone's laundry.

Make someone a playlist.

Give someone a book you think they'd like

Give someone a hug

Write a list of things you love about someone.

Wash someone's car.

Babysit, dogsit, or catsit for free.

Go out of the way to offer someone a ride.

Mow someone's lawn after mowing your own.

Send someone a care package.

Take someone to the movie.

Take someone on a spontaneous adventure.

Throw someone a surprise party.

Bring doughnuts or desserts to work.

Leave a positive sticky note on someone's desk.

Take someone out to lunch.

Lend out your umbrella when it's pouring outside.

Make two lunches for work and give one away.

Take someone to a mani, pedi, or massage.

Teach someone a recipe.

Leave quarters at the laundromat.

Pay the toll for the person behind you.

Give someone a compliment.

Leave a larger than normal tip.

Buy someone behind you in line their morning coffee.

Pay for someone's groceries behind you.

Give up a good parking spot.

Send a box of our fave donuts, bagels, or muffins to a construction site.

Smile at someone... just because (even Mother Teresa said, "We shall never know all the good that a simple smile can do.").

Hold the elevator or door open.

Put change in someone's expired parking meter (keep in mind that re-metering is illegal in some cities, especially when you are allowing them to stay beyond the time limit).

Let someone behind you at the supermarket check out first.

Send dessert to another table.

Give up your seat on the bus or subway.

Give up your window or aisle seat for someone who has a middle seat.

Bring your flight attendant some chocolates.

Help someone struggling with heavy bags.

Give someone a flower or bouquet / Bring flowers to a nursing home.

Help someone take a photo.

Take time to give someone who looks lost directions.

Stop and help someone with a flat tire.

Carry a $5 gift card with you and give it to someone randomly.

Help someone load their luggage into the overhead bin.

Give someone else the cab that you hailed.

Let someone else get seated before you at a busy restaurant.

Share your table with someone at a busy food
court.

Don't overthink your random act of kindness! Even the simplest
things can make a difference. And please share other random acts of
kindness.

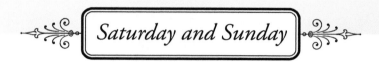

Saturday and Sunday

A joyful heart brightens one's face, but a
troubled heart breaks the spirit.

—Proverbs 15:13

Cheerfulness not only helps us thrive; it is essential for survival. We cannot successfully navigate the human condition from a dark and depressed mindset because we lose faith and hope and connection to something greater than ourselves. In this very troubling world we live in these days, we sometimes have to consciously choose to put on that smile and be positive.

It is internal cheer. It involves the attitudes we choose to cultivate inside us. Scientific evidence suggests that being happy may have major benefits for your health. For starters, being happy promotes a healthy lifestyle. It may also help combat stress, boost your immune system, protect your heart, and reduce pain. What's more—it may even increase your life expectancy.

For people who are sick, it is so easy to get depressed, lose hope, or feel frustrated. When you break a bone or get hurt and have to depend on others, it is hard to be positive every day. When we are alone and have to find our way, it is sad and sometimes painful. Cheerfulness makes almost anything bearable.

Now I know some of you are thinking, *I don't have it. I can't be that way today.* I'm telling you cheerfulness lives inside you and is always looking for an opportunity to bubble up to the surface. We can be in the deepest darkest depression and still howl with laughter at a joke or grieving an inconceivable loss and find something hysterically funny.

These moments to escape the pain and suffering remind us now that we do have cheerfulness and happiness deep inside of us at all times. Every once in a while, we "accidentally" smile or laugh at something unexpected—and that is good for us. It is good to get your internal hope, your chemistry bubbling with positive energy. Energy is contagious—positive or negative—choose cheerfulness! This world is really rough right now, and we need it.

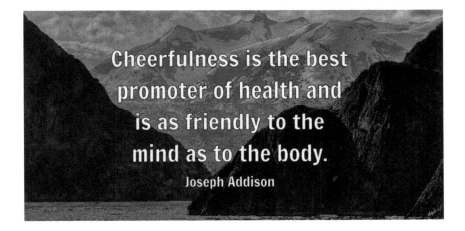

Cheerfulness is the best promoter of health and is as friendly to the mind as to the body.

Joseph Addison

Monday

The student is not above the teacher, but everyone
who is fully trained will be like their teacher.
—Luke 6:40

Teachers are some of the most selfless, giving, caring individuals in
our world. Their goals and ambitions are in seeing their students succeed in life, and many of us have our teachers to thank for where we
are! Yet teachers often face discouragement and feelings of defeat—
much like Jesus as one of his roles was that of a teacher. Some of the
ways he taught reminds me of teachers I had, whether that be in
school, at a conference, in a job, even as a volunteer.

Jesus taught with power. He knew he was doing what he was
supposed to do. That also made him a compassionate person. Does
this remind you of any teachers you know? Jesus was also very unique
and taught in different places to many different people. Sound familiar? He taught people on their level. He put people first and figured
out what they needed to get the most out of his teachings. Jesus chal-
lenged people much like our teachers and bosses and parents have
done for us. When you think of Jesus as a teacher, it can be really
encouraging. He inspired people to learn and then go out and teach.

Some people have always known they were going to teach; it's
all they ever wanted to do. Everyone can attribute some of their success to a great teacher. I had some amazing teachers in my life who
encouraged me and mentored me. My children, so far, have had
some amazing teachers as well. I have learned from them as an adult.
If you are a teacher, you know that it is not a career for the faint
of heart. You are dedicated, hardworking, and you strive to build

a joy of learning into each and every one of your students. I salute all teachers! May you be encouraged by Scripture and the way Jesus taught today and every day!

Though we are all teachers in some way, make sure you appreciate the people who have chosen the job of educating our children. Speak words of encouragement and thankfulness to the teachers you know, and it will make a difference in their day. Write these on a Post-it, send an email, or write a kind note today with Bible verses for teachers to brighten their day and show them the fruit of their hard work and dedication to their students! Also, encourage the students to do the same to get to know their teachers like their teachers are getting to know them.

Tuesday

"For the mountains may depart and the hills be removed, but my steadfast love shall not depart from you, and my covenant of peace shall not be removed," says the Lord, who has compassion on you.
—Isaiah 54:10

In order for life to be what it should, it must flow from a heart full of tenderness. The devotion we receive from God's love is undeniable. This is that quality of soul which enables us to give attention and kindness to others, to be willing and eager to do good, and to be affectionate. Like all other good qualities, this is found perfectly in the character of God.

Life without tenderness may lack holiness. As we get deeper into God, we become more tender. We feel protected, we feel we can offer warmth, kindness, and that same protection to others. This emotion, tenderness, is what we feel when we express joy and sorrow with others.

Sometimes feelings of distrust or resentment can affect our tenderness toward others. When we feel someone has misjudged us or not communicated well, we tend to allow negative thoughts to cloud our minds. Though this is the time to dig deep, focus on the needs of others. Focus on what that person may be needing.

An example of expressing tenderness is having a pet. We love them! We are affectionate with them. We protect them—until they chew your shoe, go to the bathroom in the house, etc. Then we are a little slighted in our tenderness toward them. We are irritated, feel betrayed, etc. However, they are just doing what they know, and they learn like we do when given love and training.

"Tenderness" is an emotion which expresses warm affection and seeks to share the joys and sorrows of another. God is a tender God, and the tenderness of God is sadly needed in these harsh, loveless days when tenderness is a scarce commodity among human beings. Tenderness should be an example of "unconditional love," and we need a lot more of it in our world. Try it today—judgment free day! All forgiving day! Love like God day!

Wednesday

In the beginning God created the heavens and the earth.

—Genesis 1:1

The Bible begins by telling us that all things were created by the ultimate artist, God. Additionally, from Genesis, the Bible says, "God created man in his own image." This could be interpreted as we are creators just as God created us. We create relationships, art, homes, cities, nations, and many more things including inventions even yet to be known! The creative spirit is certainly favored by God and our fellowman.

Art has been used to express how we feel as a documentation of historical events and to "simply" capture creativity. Art is the expression of human creative skill and imagination. There are many ways to express our creativity. Some people just think of paintings and sculptures; however, some people express themselves through quilting, building houses, writing novels, poetry, landscapes, inventing something, bulletin boards in the classroom—you get it!

God, with creation, has laid out the infinite number of ways for us to find and feed our creative soul! And it is important to do so. It is important to feel like you are responsible for the creation of something and feel that sense of purpose. It helps with your self-esteem and helps with encouraging someone else to continue to be creative.

I was visiting with someone recently who was looking for a job. He told me he likes to cook and do lawn work. In visiting further, the aspect he liked about both of these jobs was the same: He liked to cook because when it is good, people like it, and he was proud of what he made. He liked to do lawn work because the lawn would look better when he was done, the owner would like it, and he was proud of what he did.

Both were rewarding and great for his self-esteem and encouraging enough to do it again. Would you ever have put cooking and lawn work in the category of art?

Please check out the twelve benefits listed below. I think you will find that any list you pull up will have similar benefits and they are a great list to use in encouraging others to find their way.: Twelve Benefits of Creativity by Teach Thought: bit.ly/3eZPC8w.

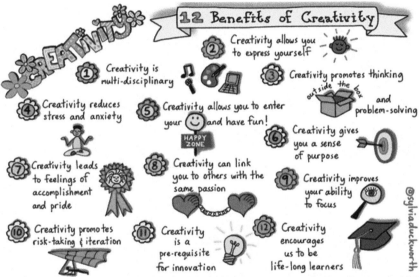

Thursday

Jesus looked at them and said, "With man this is impossible, but with God all things are possible."

—Matthew 19:26

Scripture can often be the resource we are looking for to motivate us and keep us encouraged. The inspiration and strength you need to cope with life's challenges can be found in the Bible or in devotions. If you are feeling overwhelmed, stressed, run down, even hopeless, this is a good place to start your day—reading a devotional.

Despair and anxiety have always been an intrinsic part of life on earth. In these times, we look for something to encourage us to keep going, to continue on this journey, this path we have chosen. There is always an opportunity to choose love and not let the negative energy win. You can rise above it all and be motivated to continue believing in the goodness of God and of life. Motivation is a combination of many things:

- Meditation: Time to focus is important, time for breathing and praying.
- Optimism: Positive energy is vital on your journey.
- Trusting: Trust in God.
- Imagination: Be creative, and allow yourself to dream.
- Valued: Believe in yourself! What you feel, think, and want are important.
- Affirming: Read Scripture, affirmations, devotionals—something that supports and reminds you of God's love.

- Transformative: Allow for change to take place as you grow in your trust and love for the Lord.
- Encouraging: As you motivate yourself, do the same for others.

God's plan for your life is that you have joy and live life to the fullest.

Friday

Everything should be done with dignity and in proper order.
—1 Corinthians 14:40

Many of us have heard the standard of the Proverbs 31 woman (if not, take a few minutes to read Proverbs 31:10–31). She is capable, manages her household, runs a business, cooks, and is a treasure to her husband and children. Where did she come from? I think we all strive to be more organized and be a "super" person.

It is way tougher than some people make it look though there is a purpose for having some order in our lives—for ourselves and for those around us. Simple things like setting three daily goals or planning your meals in advance can have a big impact in your life. Maybe you make a check-off list of what needs to be done. Is anyone guilty of doing things themselves because we know how we like it done? Or knowing our kids should help more, but it takes time to teach them?

It is worth it to do all of those things, and in the long run, you will be more organized and focused and free to focus on the things you choose to do.

With that in mind, here are some things you will notice:

- Decluttering and organizing clears your mind! You may actually feel renewed in energy and in spirit. It definitely reduces stress because the cause of some of our stress is the clutter.
- Some other benefits are the flexibility you will have and how creative you may become. Getting organized is not easy. No matter how dedicated you are, it doesn't mean

you have more space or more time. However, you will find both.

- Think of what a great example you are by being productive! And then you may find helpers coming along because it is freeing, fun, and makes you feel wonderful.
- You are definitely helping others when you donate things. There is a place to donate just about everything too, and someone or some company will need what you don't. So go ahead and let go of the stress of clearing the way for God's plan, and just do it.

FOR GOD IS NOT A GOD of Confusion but PEACE of

1 Corinthians 14:33

Knowing-Jesus.com

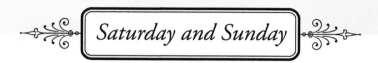

Saturday and Sunday

Again Jesus spoke to them, saying, "I am the light
of the world. Whoever follows me will not walk
in darkness, but will have the light of life."

—John 8:12

Now there is a big difference between me and God. When I name
someone, I don't have the power or the authority to make the person
fit the name. I give names in the hope and prayer that my children
will become what their names imply. But God has the right and the
power to cause anyone he names to become what the name implies.
The names he gives are sure indicators of the destiny of those he
names.

What is our calling? Do you believe in who you were meant
to be? I sometimes feel like we have to "own" it. Who are you? Can
you write down "I am..."? How many things can you say you are
and really believe it? If you are choosing peace, you must choose to
believe in yourself first.

Live into the characteristics that you say you have. If you are
kind, really be kind. Believing who you are and fulfilling God's will
is an important part of the journey of being who God created you
to be.

Don't try to be someone else. We know we are all created
uniquely. That's truly a gift from God. So let's practice the "I am"
statement. When we do, we are acknowledging God's presence in our
life. We are saying yes to being our true selves, or working on it. Be
proud of who you are, and encourage others to do the same.

Monday

> Then I will change the speech of the peoples into
> pure speech, that all of them will call on the name
> of the Lord and will serve him as one.
> —Zephaniah 3:9

In everyday life, we are content to describe things the way they appear without always going into the precise science behind what we observe. For example, we still talk about the sun rising and setting even though we know that it is the earth that revolves around the sun and not the sun that revolves around the earth. In a similar way, the Bible often uses phenomenological language to describe incredible acts of God.

The language we use to communicate with people, the expressions we make, the details we use (or don't use) all have a lot to do with how we interact with the world around us. Expressing affection through spoken affection, praise, or appreciation affects how we interact with the world around us.

The verse above refers to people using the same language and serving God in unity. Do you think it means the same language as in "all English" or the same language as in "saying the same thing"? I think we can all speak about God and his love and serving him in many different languages and still be saying the same thing.

So maybe we should learn other languages. Learning a new language allows you to learn things about a new culture, meet new people, and see new places. It can really help you open your eyes and mind to understand the world around us. After all, world peace isn't desired in our country alone.

If you are learning another language, you may be more aware of what is going on around you. You may have better focus on what is really important and relevant. One of the main goals of language is to communicate with people and to understand them. Aren't we better equipped for our journey if we are prepared to learn and understand another culture—at least the knowledge that it will be different than our own, but that maybe we have similar dreams.

Be open-minded to exploring the world around you. Think about the language that is coming from you. Are you hopeful, loving, encouraging, friendly? That's what we all should be!

Tuesday

Bear one another's burdens, and in this way
you will fulfill the law of Christ.

—Galatians 6:2

Having empathy is the ability to understand and share the feelings of another.

As Christians, we are to be imitators of God and have compassion for one another. From Scripture, we see the great empathy Jesus showed for the sick, the blind, the deaf, and more. Throughout Scripture, we are taught to humble ourselves and look at the interests of others. Try putting yourself in someone else's shoes. Bear the burden of your brothers and sisters in Christ. Always remember there is one body of Christ, but each of us make up the many parts of it.

There are three types of empathy:

- Cognitive empathy is the ability to understand how a person feels and what they might be thinking. This makes us better communicators because it helps us relay information in a way that best reaches the other person.
- Emotional empathy (also known as affective empathy) is the ability to share the feelings of another person. This type of empathy helps you build emotional connections with others.
- Compassionate empathy (also known as empathic concern) goes beyond simply understanding others and sharing their feelings; it actually moves us to take action. This is where we really do whatever we can to help others.

All these types of empathy are important in helping us be there for others.

There is a great book by Susan Verde, *I Am Human*. At first glance, you will definitely think of it as a children's book. However, I think it is for everyone. It is a hopeful meditation on being human. It reminds us that we don't do everything right all the time, but we can still make good, meaningful choices. It really celebrates empathy. I hope you'll check it out!

Love one another, and be sensitive to the feelings of others.

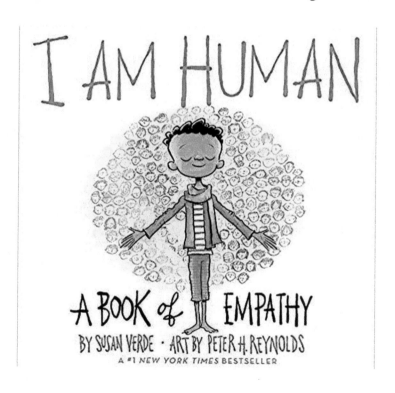

Wednesday

Many, Lord my God, are the wonders you have done, the things you planned for us. None can compare with you; were I to speak and tell of your deeds, they would be too many to declare.

—Psalm 40:5

"The wonders God has done" are what? I think of *wonder* as the things that catch your breath unexpectedly yet beautifully, something that might make you think, *Only God could create this.* Quite often, people will see something on vacation or when traveling and be in awe of the beauty of where they are: deserts, beaches, oceans, mountains, etc. And quite often, you will feel peace in those places.

Have you heard of the Seven Wonders of the World? Did you know they change? Millions of people vote on them, and they are amazing, awe-inspiring. Check out the list of the Seven Wonders of the World: bit.ly/3HBWRiY.

Think about where you have traveled in the past year? Did you see anything amazing? Something you would want to have put on a postcard? Something that God created. I think of things I have seen and feel so blessed to see such beauty and natural peace.

How can we keep that feeling of awe and of stillness right here in our everyday lives? It's hard! A lot of life is happening. It's busy. In front of us we see a messy house, weeds to pull, etc. Maybe we need to look at things in a new way:

- My messy house: glorious shelter for someone
- My weedy flower bed: holds beautiful flowers
- My pile of laundry: clothing for someone

- My dusty bookshelf: books to read for someone who loves knowledge and desires an education

What does your list look like?

Sometimes, wonder is all around us. The glorious work of God is everywhere!

Thursday

For the Spirit God gave us does not make us timid,
but gives us power, love and self-discipline.
—2 Timothy 1:7

The Bible warns us that if we do not have self-control, we will be slaves to what controls us. Food, lust, money, our words—we can find ourselves overwhelmed with the consequences of not having self-control in many areas of life. Having self-control is the very foundation for living a life of righteousness and selflessness that reflects Jesus and brings glory to God. We have the power to bring sins under control! We have the power to choose to be self-disciplined in all areas of our lives, which also means we can choose not to be! These choices really do have an effect on everything surrounding our lives.

If you or someone you know is struggling with self-control. it's time to change that. It's time to enjoy the benefits of having it and let go of the effects of not having it. We often think of how the lack of discipline has an effect on us; eating too much junk food, staying up too late, driving over the speed limit, saying things we shouldn't have. These negative emotions and impulses can have a lasting effect on us—it's contagious energy.

There needs to be a balance of self-control in our lives. If we have too little, we may have no motivation, no goals, no will power; we're quick to blame anyone for our shortcomings. However, if we have too much, we can't relax, we are distant from people, we might not take risks in which we aren't in control completely—so balance is good here.

So how do we find that balance, you ask? We relax, breathe, and believe. Learn to plan a little, and figure out what *you* want. A lot of our lack of self-control is due to taking care of what someone else wants. Really try to get healthy: physically (good stress relief), emotionally (be good to you), mentally (know the consequences of your lack of discipline), and spiritually (read some scriptures or devotionals). Self-control plays a major role in our lives, and it is often a big factor in our overall levels of satisfaction.

You all chose to receive this devotional—that's a big commitment. It's also a good plan on helping you take care of yourself. It's also taking up some of your time. Hopefully, you have had some self-discipline and figured out a way to make it work for you and not against you. The steps to make this happen are a great example of what you need to do for other areas you want to focus on as well—and don't be too hard on yourself. It takes practice and consistency.

Friday

Our mouths were filled with laughter, our tongues
with songs of joy. Then it was said among the nations,
"The Lord has done great things for them."
—Psalm 126:2

God designs creation to teach us, but he also uses it to assure us, lighten our spirits, or make us smile. Laughing is such an amazing gift God gave us. Not only does it help you cope with sadness and everyday life, it also helps ease stress and tension. Have you ever felt mad and then someone said something to make you laugh? Even though you were upset, the laughter made your heart feel better.

When you think about some of God's creations, like an anteater for example, God must have had a sense of humor, right? Poor thing—this long thin snout only eats ants! What about Jesus? Well, don't you think turning water to wine at a wedding celebration was pretty fun! Remembering that there was joy in his life makes him more relatable to us as a person. It is important to remember that in all the trials that come along in our lives, we should only take some things so serious. After all, there is some purpose, whether we figured it out or not, and we will get there.

If you can laugh about something, especially yourself, then you can forgive yourself and forgive others. If you can forgive others, you can accept others and their differences and move forward in the quest for peace. Laughter is such an important tool in healing not just for ourselves but for everyone. It can help with heartache, help with depression, help with pain.

There are many stories, articles, books, comedians, pictures, etc., that help us laugh. They teach us to laugh and teach us about laughter in our lives. A common thread in all of them is being able to laugh at ourselves or with our friends. Laughing at church is actually okay! And it feels great—speaking from personal experience here—my children and my husband tend to make me laugh right when I am about to "lay down the law" about listening to the pastor. Honestly, it feels great. I still get the message and probably get more of it because I am no longer focusing on what my kids are doing or not doing.

Here is a prayer I found in a book I have, *Laugh Out Loud* by Women of Faith (Thomas Nelson):

> Protect me from knowing what I don't need to know.
> Protect me from even knowing that there are things to know that I don't know.
> Protect me from knowing that I decided not to know about the things that I decided not to know about.
> Amen.
>
> Lord, protect me from the consequences of the above prayer. (Douglas Adams)

I love the message of this prayer. We worry so much and spend so much time *not* enjoying life because we worry about the unknown. Rather than worry, give it to God. Trust that there is a plan, and you are not alone.

Share a smile today!

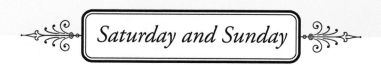

Saturday and Sunday

> Very early in the morning, while it was still dark, Jesus got up,
> left the house and went off to a solitary place, where he prayed.
> —Mark 1:35

Praying can help people come to a greater understanding of God's purpose for their lives. They usually think the response they might get to their prayers is "God answers prayers, but not always in the way the person wants."

Daily devotionals are publications which provide a specific spiritual reading for each calendar day. They are affirmations about various things that we want to focus on. They are scriptures, pictures, prayers, songs, ways to connect, etc.

Devotions and prayers help people connect to God. Sometimes, taking the time to pray, read some scripture, and talk to God is what we need to reevaluate circumstances in our lives. Devotion also means a commitment or dedication to some purpose. Your devotion may be your commitment to recycling; however, let people read their paper first. Maybe you are dedicated to peace. Devotions can also be related to offering our prayers to God.

Whatever this is for you, it's valuable and important. Please look at this to see other ways we benefit from devotions: Six Benefits of Ordinary Daily Devotions: bit.ly/34pOZ6x.

Monday

I can do all things through him who strengthens me.
—Philippians 4:13

This verse is well-known for being a spiritual boost of self-confidence that can be applied to any ambition or aspiration in life. The Bible actually has quite a bit to say about self-confidence, self-worth, and self-respect. God provides us with strength and all that we need to live a godly life.

As we grow in faith, our confidence in God grows. He is always there for us. When we're looking for direction, God gives us the self-assurance we need to walk the path he has provided for us.

I believe that in todays' world, confidence is found in many different ways: in status, relationships, money, cars, houses, clothes, beauty, careers, achievements, education, goals, popularity, number of friends or followers you have, etc. Though that is not confidence that will stick with us, it is temporary and can eventually lead to a lack of self-confidence.

God will not let you down, so focus on yourself and not all the other things to gain your self-confidence. Believing in yourself is far more valuable than having a million followers or the biggest house. Many of us don't believe in ourselves maybe from fear of not living up to someone else's expectations, maybe for fear of failing. Trust, and take a leap of faith. The confidence that comes with it will surprise you!

I found this article/list of twenty-five actions to boost your self-confidence. I found it on zenhabits.net: bit.ly/3q1jSGn.

I am sharing this for a couple reasons—I loved it! And you will notice not one of these twenty-five actions requires a bunch of money, friends, etc.—just us deciding to believe in ourselves.

Even a close friend or family member can say something that brings you down without ever meaning to. Sometimes we compare ourselves to others when we shouldn't. That is why God is giving you self-confidence. He never fails. You are uniquely you!

Tuesday

My teaching will fall like raindrops; my speech will settle like dew—
like gentle rains on grass, like spring showers on all that is green.
—Deuteronomy 32:2

Tenderness is gentleness and kindness. Tenderness is a feeling of concern, affection, or warmth. It's the quality of a person who cries when they see someone get hurt or who gently picks up a tiny kitten, someone who cries when something great and caring happens or reassures a lost child that things are okay.

This is that quality of soul which enables us to give kind attention to others, to be willing and eager to do good, to be careful what we say to people. Like all other good qualities, this is found in perfection in the character of God. God exhibited a lot of tenderness in his creations. We can do the same.

Tender means "to be delicate, sensitive, soft-hearted." Forget about bad stuff; instead, focus on the good things in life. I know this is easier said than done. It's natural to be more protective and defensive, but it is okay and necessary to be forgiving and more compassionate.

Be good to yourself while you are being good to others. Find a place to recharge your heart when you are using it so much. This might be a library, the couch, a park, a pool—someplace you can pray, release the anxiousness that comes with all the yuck in the world. This will help you feel refreshed and ready to be compassionate.

There is an overwhelming amount of hate, ignorance, and injustice in the world, and our hearts want to make it right. We all have the ability to sort through the daily "trash" and try to find the treasures in it. We can pour love and forgiveness and righteousness and gentleness and beauty out into the world. Sometimes, fighting for this peace isn't what everyone wants. You see the anger and frustration on social media—and it accomplishes nothing. So keep up the "good" fight, and don't give up!

Wednesday

Share with the Lord's people who are in need. Practice hospitality.
—Romans 12:13

Practice hospitality. What do you do to practice hospitality? Do you donate clothes to help people who need them? Do you donate food to the various food banks for people who are hungry? Do you give money to the person with the cardboard sign on the corner?

Hospitality is defined as "the friendly and generous reception and entertainment of guests, visitors, or strangers." So do you say hi to the new person at church or in school or in a job? Do you make them feel welcome? Invite them to coffee?

Hospitality can cover a lot of ground and is intentional but not—it should come natural, but sometimes we have to work at it. Sometimes people are hospitable based on judgment, but that's not part of the definition. My son tends to have a soft spot for people on the corners. He really wants to know why they are there, what happened to get them where they are and is happy to give them his own money. However, he doesn't like to give money to people who have a beer in their pocket or if they are right by the liquor store. He doesn't mean to judge them; he just cares enough that he doesn't think that is what's going to help them.

One of my Pastor's wife sometimes has sandwiches in her car and Ziplocs of dog food to give to people. That might be an answer for my son to feel he is giving something nourishing to people. I'm grateful that he cares, but we have to cultivate a mentality that we help those in need and try not judge what they need.

What about new people—if someone is coming to church or a new job, they are in need of hospitality. They are already nervous, hoping to meet people, looking for something different in their life. Be radical and say hi. Ask them where they are from. We are all created in the image of God. We should all work and be together in this world and try to be welcoming!

Practice hospitality!

Thursday

For just as each of us has one body with many members, and these members do not all have the same function, so in Christ we, though many, form one body, and each member belongs to all the others.
—Romans 12:4–5

The idea of community comes from the sense of responsibility we have for each other. In the Bible, God encourages us to take care of each other while following the Word of the Lord. In our homes, we are encouraged to believe that family is important. In school, we may be encouraged to believe that friends are important. All are important, and all boil down to community.

Maintaining a connection with God, our families, our friends, even strangers is how we ensure a thriving community. Community can be described as having a common union with other people. The Bible says the Holy Spirit is present whenever believers gather together. God intended for us to thrive in relationship with others.

It's important to spend time alone with God, soaking up his Word, but he didn't intend for us to live in isolation. He specifically designed us to crave—and thrive in—relationship with others.

Community is so supportive. To have the encouragement of the people around you is wonderful. We can learn from each other and lift each other up. It can also be a lot of fun! Being with people who have something in common should be enjoyable. Go to church together or a book study with your friends, a ball game—all sorts of "community" helps people to grow in love.

Community is life giving. We're our best selves when we're experiencing life's highs and lows with other believers. Everyone needs community—no exclusions. When you commit to being in community with people daily, that's where you will really see ministry happening. It is definitely a sign of a mature faith. For the last ninety days, we have been in community together reading these devotions. We've been growing our faith with a group of people from all over the country, many we don't even know. Yet it worked.

Because at the end of the day, when we grow in our relationships with others, we're growing in relationship with him!

Friday

For I know the plans I have for you," declares
the LORD, "plans to prosper you and not to harm
you, plans to give you hope and a future.
—Jeremiah 29:11

I personally really like this scripture, a reminder from God that there is a plan and that things will be okay, so don't give up—have hope. To hope is to want something to happen or be true and actually think that it could happen or be true, a feeling that there is a reason to keep trying, keep doing, keep smiling, keep loving, keep choosing! Where there is hope, other positive emotions such as courage and confidence and happiness emerge, and those emotions are our coping strategy—they help us keep going.

Honestly, hope usually arises when things are really, really bad. It's during difficult times that we discover the possibilities that are still present, and hope appears. When we have hope, we are able to move beyond the fear and the pain. We are able to stay above water when we are drowning in worry and sadness. When we have hope and courage, we can be more creative in our problem solving and retain our optimism; and having a positive outlook helps us survive our journey, whichever journey we are on right now.

Some people are on tougher journeys than others like fighting a disease, being in an abusive relationship, finding a job, fighting Mother Nature, etc. I don't know how someone draws the strength for those things sometimes, but I bet *hope* has something to do with it. It allows us to move past and know there is more—there is a better day.

Having hope propels us to achieve our dreams and drives us forward toward our pursuits. Hope is the light at the end of the tunnel, the northern star that guides us on our journey. We all carry hope for each other in different ways. Your smile to a stranger may be the hope they need to know there is kindness in the world.

The poem below is a great listing of many things that we could only hope for in the world. There are things that are the way they are meant to be, and we can't change them. We can, however, have hope to make some changes happen, make progress toward a different reality, and having things we hope for is why we continue to follow the journey that God has planned for us.

If Only...

If Only...
A prayer was held in our nation,
Beauty was seen in more ways than one,
Children who are lost could find their salvation,
Death was slain and torture was done.

If Only...
Earth was awakened after years of endurance,
Forgotten feelings were rekindled anew,
God was man's only path and assurance,
Hope was the foundation of the world we knew.

If Only...
I knew more stories than those that were told,
Joy was a plague, and peace a disease,
Knowledge was worth more than silver and gold,
Love was sacred and endless as the seas.

If Only...
Miracles were seen more than daylight,
Never was replaced with forever,
Our eyes could see through the dark of the night,
Passion lived in us more than ever.

If Only...
Questions were answered, and answers were
    questioned,
Roses were pure and without thorns,
Sadness received only love and affection,
The empty knew why it was they were born.

If Only...
Us as a nation would join hands in song,
Victory was a gift to the humble,
When tears were shed, the earth felt strong,
Exalted men would fall and crumble.

If Only...
You and I would last forever.

If Only...

Source: bit.ly/3JkakNy

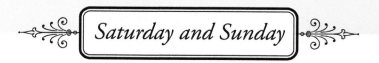
Saturday and Sunday

May the Lord of peace himself give you peace always
in every way. The Lord be with all of you.
—2 Thessalonians 3:16

When we are choosing to find peace, we don't have to look any far-
ther than ourselves. We find it through the example we set. We need
to show kindness, goodness, compassion, light—many things that
the world in which we live needs more. We must direct our energy
right here and start with us.

Living in the moment is your ticket to choosing peace, finding
your happiness and contentment in a world full of discontent and
turmoil. Pray for people, things, the world, and then turn the TV/
electronics/social media off and live today. When you are happy, the
world is happy. When you are at peace, the world is at peace. Some
say "the present is called present because it is a gift."

Live in the moment. Have gratitude for everything. We should
be acknowledging life, health, our families, our friends, the things we
do, the mind we have, everything about us. Stay true to yourself—
you are amazing! And when you are happy, you make others around
you happy. You create peace.

Have a caring attitude, and be helpful. Share your beautiful
smile with others. Brighten their day. Make time for the people you
love. Spend time with them. They have much to offer you and will
"refill your cup" when you need it. Be generous and giving. What
you will receive in return will be more valuable than you can imagine. You will change lives, and you will feel amazing.

Please take care of yourself. Allow rest, retreats, time for what makes you balanced and complete. Do something for yourself today. Maybe you take a nap, buy a new outfit, take a nature hike. Do it. Breathe in the world around you. You are where peace begins—one person at a time. Do what you were called to do today. Choose *peace*.

Traci Keck is a "typical" busy woman: wife, mom, sister, aunt, friend, employee, business owner, volunteer, housekeeper, chef, chauffeur, planner, shopper—you get it! What sets her apart is her never-ending desire to spread positive energy in the world—for real! She is a cup-half-full, silver-lining, something-good-will-come-out-of-this type of girl—sometimes rather annoyingly.

She was raised by a single mom of six. Her version is she had a strong, independent mom who worked endlessly to get through life, take care of her children, and loved with all her soul—period. Traci learned from her mom that God doesn't give you more than you can handle. She learned from her twin, Staci, that God indeed has a plan and doesn't leave anyone out, and she has chosen to believe those principles *always*.

Her love is her family: her husband (Ron) and kids (Coleman, Jordi, and Gracie Boots), and she is inspired by them daily! She feels so grateful to have the family, friends, and connections that are in her life; though, like so many, she still lives real-life struggles. She makes mistakes; she's made some wrong choices, and too much negative energy can sink her. And no matter how much negative energy is floating around in this world of ours, she tries to find something positive in everything. It is the way she is wired and has been her whole life.

Traci first started writing devotions to help herself find ways to find the good, the purpose, the positive. She was looking at what God makes available in life and then at the choices we can make. She found relating Scripture to real-life experiences gave her hope. She also found that in sharing her stories, she wasn't alone—most of the world was trying to figure this life out. Traci quickly learned that sharing devotions, helping others find hope today gave her a sense of purpose—purpose that helped her spread positive energy in the world. Her hope is that you will find the hope, love, and strength you need today—so you can choose again tomorrow.

CPSIA information can be obtained
at www.ICGtesting.com
Printed in the USA
BVHW090019280423
663158BV00019B/741